Cambridge Studies in Social Anthropology

General Editor: Jack Goody

MW01049977

64

COSMOLOGIES IN THE MAKING

A sacred meal where initiates and ancestors share the meat from a sacred hunt, in an ancestral temple in Bolovip village area.

Cosmologies in the making:

A generative approach to cultural variation in inner New Guinea

FREDRIK BARTH
Ethnographic Museum, University of Oslo

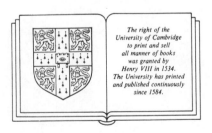

The right of the
University of Cambridge
to print and sell
all manner of books
was granted by
Henry VIII in 1534.
The University has printed
and published continuously
since 1584.

CAMBRIDGE UNIVERSITY PRESS

Cambridge
New York   Port Chester   Melbourne   Sydney

Published by the Press Syndicate of the University of Cambridge
The Pitt Building, Trumpington Street, Cambridge CB2 1RP
40 West 20th Street, New York, NY 10011, USA
10 Stamford Road, Oakleigh, Melbourne 3166, Australia

First published 1987
First paperback edition 1989

Printed in Great Britain at the University Press, Cambridge

British Library cataloguing in publication data

Barth, Fredrik
Cosmologies in the making: a generative
approach to cultural variation in inner New Guinea.—
(Cambridge studies in social anthropology).
1. Ethnology—Papua New Guinea
2. Papua New Guinea—Social conditions
I. Title
306'.0995   GN671.N5

Library of Congress cataloguing in publication data

Barth, Fredrik, 1928–
Cosmologies in the making.
(Cambridge studies in social anthropology; no. 64)
Bibliography.
Includes index.
1. Ok (Papua New Guinea people)—Social life and customs.
2. Ethnology—Papua New Guinea.
3. Social change—Case studies.
4. Culture diffusion—Case studies.
5. Papua New Guinea—Social life and customs.
I. Title. II. Series.
DU740.42.B36   1987   306'.0899912   87-8001

ISBN 0 521 34279 1 hard covers
ISBN 0 521 38735 3 paperback

Contents

Foreword

Symbols and knowledge

Fredrik Barth needs no introduction from me. He is already justly well known for his series of ethnographic studies on four different continents, which he has combined with an interest in theoretical problems relating constructively to his empirical enquiries. But I agreed to introduce the present volume both because the particular problem he analyses is one which goes to the heart of the comparative analysis of human interaction among neighbouring peoples, especially in societies without writing, and because it is a question that has also been one of my own implicit concerns. Like Barth in New Guinea, in West Africa I was struck by the degree of similarity that occurred between the economic, linguistic, and to some extent, cultural aspects of LoDagaa society and that of the peoples surrounding them, while at the same time there was a great diversity in other elements, especially the religious and magico-ritual domains. In the latter there were the same kinds of dramatic variation that Barth found among the mountain Ok, where, as he points out, the differences are apparent not just to external observers, but, some of them, indeed, shock the actors themselves, who view them as not merely 'ungrammatical', but as actually objectionable. Other differences are more neutral, while yet others are tacit (that is, un-perceived or unelaborated). But none of these differences is simply 'symbolic', however deeply felt; rather they involve differences in bodies of knowledge 'about the world'. Even 'the major modes in which religious and cosmological ideas are expressed' differ between mountain Ok communities. And the fact that their languages have not greatly diverged suggests that such variations have emerged in a relatively short time period.

The problem Barth tackles in this book is how best to approach a situation of this kind. Anthropology's historical emphasis on fieldwork, and on functional or structural analysis, has meant that, unlike the comparative approach adopted by Frazer and his contemporaries, beliefs and practices have subsequently tended to be analysed solely in terms of a cultural system. The basic pro-cedures of such analysis involve first making a series of functional or logical models which can be interwoven, then, second, constructing a single model which can generate the different forms. But, Barth suggests, if one wants to look at a wider range of data, the approaches available in contemporary anthropology are very limited. Indeed, this limitation applies even internally to a particular system. For all variants of functional and structural models assume a high degree of order, of unity, either in terms of their isomorphy with other aspects of the socio-cultural system, or with respect to an underlying model. From this standpoint the substance of local variation is essentially ignored.

For Barth, on the contrary, internal variations provide an entry into the actual processes by which wider 'cultural' variations occur. We need to examine these internal variations carefully if we are 'to get our ontological assumptions right'; that is, to make a realistic analysis of the changes we can reasonably expect to take place. That means not only making an appeal to *bricolage* (as Lévi-Strauss has done) or to creativity (as I have done – wanting to set the general cognitive process in a wider transcultural context), but also examining the use and elaboration of metaphor (as any literary critic might predict). For 'ritual builds on metaphor'; or, to put it more concretely, and perhaps more generally, leading actors in ritual and myth elaborate the performance, partly because in oral societies there can be little precise verbatim transmission of complex thought or action, especially when this is thought or acted intermittently.

Consequently, we find a situation where as Barth puts it, 'the cultural content' of Ok cosmology is distributed between 'many sub-traditions located in numerous villages and temples' which are 'further subject to a constant oscillation between public performance and personal safekeeping in the care of a small number of ritual experts'. Clearly, in this light, what is called 'culture', as distinct from its sub-traditions, tends to be arbitrary. And since in conditions of creativity, 'culture' is always 'in the making' and rarely a set of collective representations in the sense that much sociology and anthropology assume, the distinction between the social and the personal, the cultural and the individual, becomes more blurred. Indeed, the very concept of a culture as a tidy bundle of meaningful traditions handed down by a particular social group must be open to question, except for relatively small and isolated groups. And even among the latter, the processes of communication both within and between generations act in generative ways, creating variants which are not simply substitutes, except in a purely formal sense, of what went on before.

While we can describe this as a process of 'subjectification', it is also one of the 'objectification', of developing the possibilities inherent not only in a specific cultural situation, but in the human condition itself, especially in its creative manipulation of linguistic concepts. An analysis of this process is advanced not so much by the examination of 'logical' as of empirical and historical transformations.

The way in which different interpretations are developed or constrained is

viii

well illustrated in Barth's discussion of the varying uses of the concepts of water and the wild boar in ritual situations, as metaphors and as instruments in the communication and development of knowledge. These variations sometimes develop of 'inherent' characteristics of these natural features and sometimes assign them more 'arbitrary' meanings. But their cognitive potentialities are elaborated by various ritual exponents, giving rise to subtraditions and cultural differences.

Barth compares the development of such variations with the emergence of different traditions within a scholarly field, that of social anthropology itself. The comparison may seem far-fetched, but it is important to stress that differences must emerge by some general mechanism that operates throughout the range of human societies. For there are times when ritual specialists in oral cultures are involved in activities essentially similar to those of a poet or novelist in our own (albeit always allowing for differences in context as well as of media).

Only by recognizing the process of creativity can one bypass the overdetermined notions of the nature of human interaction that fail to account either for internal changes or for external differences. In many parts of the world, considerable variations, especially in the religious action of oral cultures, occur between neighbouring groups, alongside great similarities in other domains. This situation in a small corner of Highland New Guinea is Barth's starting point. Similar circumstances exist in northern Ghana, where Fortes drew attention, as Barth has done, to the very different attitudes towards aspects of sexuality in two neighbouring groups, despite the apparent similarity of relations between men and women therein. In myth and ritual the differences were yet more marked. When I first recorded a version of the Bagre, Fortes thought he might have missed a recitation of this kind among the Hill Tallis. But in fact these long recitations of a 'mythical' kind are distributed very unevenly over the cultural landscape of West Africa, as they are among the Ok, and there is every reason to regard them as specific products of a specific set of localized circumstances which, building upon more general elements, then come to characterize one set of people rather than another. Not a 'culture' in the Ghanaian case, but the members of the association that cuts across 'cultural' boundaries, such as they are. Many of these variations, as Barth stresses, cannot be seen as 'isomorphic differences' between societies. On the other hand, the existence of such long myths, for example, may in some cases have consequences for the organization of society (as Barth argues in the case with certain forms of ancestor worship); in other instances the variations may be related to differences in social organization that could well be regarded as 'prior'; and in yet others there may be little or no link with social organizational features. A satisfactory theoretical scheme has to allow, willy nilly, for all three types of relation between the variables.

The process of trying to specify, define and analyse the nature of cultural transmission also raises the question of the more general differences between western and non-western traditions of knowledge. Here, as Barth suggests, the mode of communication is significant. It is not simply a matter of distinguishing the West from the rest. For example, in India, the twin processes of universalism and parochialization, identified by Redfield and others with the Great and Little Traditions, are associated respectively with the written and oral as the dominant channel of communication.

The nature of the media is relevant too in the tendency of the Baktaman, whom Barth also studied, to 'locate personally remembered events in terms of space – where they happened – rather than time – when they happened', reflecting, he suggests, 'the absence of any calendrical system for naming points in time'. While not necessarily connected with writing *per se*, this feature is closely linked, as I have suggested elsewhere, to the existence of graphic representation, to the absence of 'measurement', a point Barth stresses also when talking about the development of 'a universal science' as 'an elaborate tradition of knowledge built on consistency, generalisation, deduction, experiment and measurement' (p. 68). Again, the processes of generalization and abstraction, while not, of course, confined to societies with writing, are greatly extended by the ability to write.

Finally, the influence of the means of communication is seen at another very general level. Barth's argument is concerned with the circumstances of 'the storage in the individual mind, without literary aids, of complex cultural materials over a long time, followed by a demand for their manifestation in complex and vital performance of mystery cults', a process which 'must be highly evocative of personal involvement by the ritual expert in the cultural symbols in his keeping, and could be expected to result in his marginally reshaping them in form and content, in harmony with his own visions, at every new performance' (p. 30). This situation is clearly different from those in which a written text exists. At one level a published text, just because it is made 'public', does away with secrecy. Even when the text is restricted to the priesthood, while obviously excluding neither oral embellishments nor written commentaries, it does provide a point of reference for instruction and for control. 'Authorized versions' inevitably push creativity into other channels.

Secret knowledge is not exclusive to the oral register, but it is encouraged by it, especially where only a few individuals are thought to hold that knowledge in their memory store. And the fact that it is they rather than a text who are seen as responsible for its retention and reproduction is at the heart of the nature of the process of 'cultural genetics'. Not only does the mind fail to store such material in verbatim form over long (or even over relatively short) periods, but the absence of texts means that ideas of what is the same and what is not take on a different perspective. Notions of 'truth' depend upon the touchstone.

The question with which Barth is, as I have been, concerned is not only of

Foreword

storage, of retention, but of reproduction – by whom and under what circumstances. Whether or not the 'knowledge' is held by one or more individuals, what matters more is who reproduces it in the ceremonial situation. In this context the recitation is neither a repetition nor yet an alternative 'reading', but an authoritative statement for all those present which they themselves will modify and elaborate in their turn. What matters culturally is what is transmitted. Silent knowledge is lost knowledge. The spoken continues rather than endures – in similar forms in the versions of one reciter, and with greater modifications when the next reciter takes up the duty of 'memorizing', reconstructing, and reproducing the utterance. We fail to understand the nature of this knowledge if we view it in fixed, textual terms, even as an underlying 'structure' of an architectural kind – the metaphor is inappropriate to the generative process involved, adequate as it may be for linguistics in the more restricted sense. The *parole/langue* distinction may be satisfactory for the basic linguistic 'code', but it is too restrictive for what you do with words.

On one level this process of transmission is connected with the problem of the *loss* of knowledge as well as its increment, the danger of entropy involved in 'guarding knowledge and revealing it only slowly and late in the life of new men' (p. 48). Since knowledge is held largely in the minds of men, rather than being stored in a book or a computer, the older are inevitably at once the most experienced, and the most privileged communicators, as well as the most likely to die, taking their knowledge with them to the world of the ancestors. The dead must therefore know more than the living; the forefathers are also the forebearers, the carriers of 'tradition'. And it is in the cult of the ancestors that the dead reveal some of their superior, more comprehensive, knowledge.

Barth's concern not simply with systems of knowledge at any one point in time and space, but with their distribution among individuals, and the existence and generation of variants (and sometimes similarities) both within and between social groups, raises fundamental questions about the nature of 'culture' which have been glossed over, set aside, or misunderstood, by many theorists and analysts. His text is one I urge the reader to read with great attention, for it makes an important contribution to these issues, even if much still remains to be done in the field of comparative studies, which in turn will redirect in more specific, more productive channels the intensive work of the field ethnographer.

Jack Goody

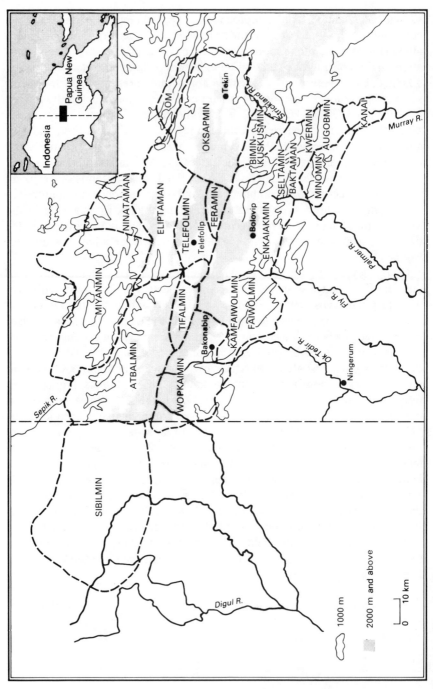

Major territories of the mountain Ok

1

The problem

The great proliferation of ritual forms, cult organizations, and social structures found among the Mountain Ok provides a challenge to anthropological description, explanation, and theory. This extended essay is an attempt to analyse variations in ritual between cognate and contiguous Mountain Ok communities in a way that will provide insights into the forms of religion and society in an area, and raise theoretical questions as to how these can best be perceived and analysed.

Thus, the object of study in this analysis is not demarcated and conceptualized as 'a culture' but as a variety of culture – specifically, the varieties of cosmological ideas and expressions in a population of 'neolithic' cultivators and hunters in a recently contacted area of Inner New Guinea. To promote clarity of expression I shall sometimes use the term 'sub-tradition' to refer to the ideas which members of a local community or a single language group regard as true, and 'tradition' for the conglomerate stream of ideas and symbols of a plurality of genetically related and intercommunicating communities. These are not analytical but descriptive terms in my effort to account for how Ok ideas vary and are distributed between individuals, congregations, and local areas.

My focus is on the analysis of the content of this aggregate tradition of knowledge: the (variety of) ideas it contains, and how they are expressed; the pattern of their distribution, within communities and between communities; the processes of (re)production in this tradition of knowledge, and how they may explain its content and pattern of distribution; thus, the processes of creativity, transmission and change.

The main purpose of my effort is to develop the theoretical framework for this discourse. I cannot expect others to be as captivated by the particulars of the imagery and ideas of Ok peoples as I am after what I have experienced among them. So, in the tradition of most social anthropological writing, the main thrust is theoretical, not descriptive: I wish to contribute to the development of a comparative anthropology of knowledge. But again in conformity with that tradition, I attempt to develop such theory in constant confrontation with empirical data: I subscribe to a methodology that meets the challenge of fitting theory to the broadest possible range of facts.

1

Cosmologies in the making

As a consequence of this hierarchy of purposes, the organization of the following text is one where I shift between sketches of data which serve to pose a problem, theoretical discussions which seek to develop a perspective on that problem, and further marshalling of data to illustrate or test what the theoretical proposals can and cannot achieve. This format has the drawback that the reader may feel at a disadvantage, suspecting that I produce bits of data and bits of theory only as these are most convenient for my argument. On the other hand, the sympathetic reader will recognize that a less tailored presentation would have other drawbacks in making the detailed ethnography even less accessible and its relation to the pro-and-contra arguments more opaque.

My point of departure is my own work in 1969 among the Baktaman (Barth 1975) – a Mountain Ok community of 185 inhabitants. Against a background of their daily life and activities I sought to describe their sacred symbols, cult activities and beliefs with special reference to their male initiations, and thereby to provide the lineaments of a secret and compelling world view characterizable as a mystery cult of fertility, growth, and ancestral blessing.

By 1983, about a dozen anthropologists have worked among cognate groups, and my wife and I have revisited for about three months' further work in the area in 1981/82.[1] There is thus a scattering of comparative material from a total population of c. 15,000 individuals, of six closely related language communities, occupying c. 10,000 km^2 of upland forests and mountains. In most outer respects, this population is reasonably homogeneous: technology, subsistence and economy are closely similar, based on shifting horticulture with an emphasis on taro, extensive hunting and collecting of forest and streambed products, and the raising of domestic pigs. Languages are closely cognate, physical type is indistinguishable. House type and dress are so similar that, apart from a few indicative details, photographs from one village could be used to illustrate life in another.

Despite this common base, religious practices and beliefs vary dramatically

[1] This revisit took place through the kind offices of the Institute of Papua-New Guinea Studies, and was financed by the Provincial Government of the Western Province, Papua-New Guinea.

The main sources for the materials on which I have built are thus the following (for references, see bibliography):

Regional: Barth, F. 1971 and field notes from 1967, 1968, and 1982. Craig, B. 1981. Pouwer, J. 1964.
Baktaman: Barth, F. 1975 and field notes from 1968, 1982.
Bimin-Kuskusmin: Poole, F.J.P. various published and unpublished writings.
Bolovip: Barth, F. field notes from 1982.
Imigabip: Jones, B.A. 1980.
Mianmin: Gardner, D.S. 1983.
Telefolmin: Craig, B. and Jorgensen, D.W. various published and unpublished writings.
Tifalmin: Wheatcroft, W. 1976.
Wopkaimin: Barth, F. field notes from 1982. Hyndman, D.C. various published and unpublished writings.

The problem

as between groups and communities. Let me give some examples of this variation, to indicate the kinds of materials with which we are confronted and thereby the kinds of problems that arise.

Skulls as concrete symbols

All Ok people seem to practice what may be characterized as a cult of ancestors, using skulls and bones of the deceased as sacred relics.

Among the Baktaman, I found major relics located in two kinds of temples: a temple for hunting trophies and sacrifices for taro increase, in which also senior men reside (*Katiam*), and a non-residential temple for warfare and taro increase rites (*Yolam*). Clan ancestors, represented by fingerbones, clavicles, breastbones and mandibles contained in string bags are found in the various *Katiam* (*Kati*-house', etymology unknown) temples; and skulls, skull fragments, and long bones are located in the central *Yolam* ('Ancestor-house') temple. For the last twenty years at least, only *one* complete skull has served as the focal relic, placed against the inner wall between the two sacred fires. Though this skull is known to be of a particular clan, it symbolizes and represents the category of all ancestors; cult observances are directed towards this ancestor for all different ritual purposes and his forehead is painted white, red, or both, according to the nature of the occasion. There is no necessary connection between the clan of the presiding ritual leader and that of the relic, and the members of all other clans, despite their descent from ancestors deriving from separate events of creation, address their prayers to ancestors to this common relic and share their sacrificial meals with him.

In Bolovip, 30 km to the west within the same language group, where I spent a month in 1982, there are five skulls of four different clans in the central *Yolam* (and there are also two other *Yolams* in this large, residentially divided community). The skulls are divided into two distinct groups, placed to the right and to the left respectively: two are *imename* (*imen* = taro) and three are *wúname* (*wún* = arrow). The former are used collectively for taro and fertility cult only, and are painted with a white line on their foreheads; the latter are for warfare cult and are painted red only; no skull should be painted both white *and* red (I return below, pp. 51f. to the deeper significance of this rule). The ritual leader, and other initiated persons present for ceremonies and sacrifices, must only present prayers and offerings to the skull of their own clan; or if their own clan is not represented among the skulls, then only to the skull of their mother's clan, or that of their father's mother.

All such information, and entrance to the cult houses, are strictly limited to appropriately initiated men: knowledge and participation are treated as terrible and vital secrets. Fortunately, word of my initiation among the Baktaman thirteen years earlier had spread to Bolovip, so I was allowed into these inner sanctuaries and could collect detailed information despite the shortness of my

3

visit. Sitting in the temple one evening, I was told with a mixture of sensationalism and disgust: 'You will not believe this, but we are not lying: In Imigabip (the neighbouring community, 10 km to the west) they have a *female* skull in their temple!' Use of female skulls is also confirmed for Telefolmin (Craig 1981). Among the Bimin-Kuskusmin, only 30 km (of very rough terrain) north of the Baktaman, indeed, their ethnographer (Poole 1976) reports the crucial place of broken female skulls among the sacra also of the clan temples!

Mafom initiation

Other dimensions of contrast may be illustrated with respect to major symbolism in initiations. A widely distributed initiation among Mountain Ok (and indeed also among peoples of other language families south-west of the Ok areas) centres on the construction of elaborate pandanus wigs for the novices, and the use of red body paint. This initiation, called *Mafomnang* among the Baktaman, occurs as the fourth step in their series of initiations. The red paint for the occasion is made of a secret mixture of red ochre, the juice of the large red pandanus fruit (*P. conoideus*), and a strongly red-staining bark extract, mixed with a base of melted pig's fat from a sacrificed village pig. The result is applied to the face and body of each novice, and the 'male' part of the wig, leaving the 'female' part of the wig as the only unpainted part of the novice.

The Bimin-Kuskusmin have a similar complex of pandanus wig, red colour, and fat associated with their sixth, seventh and ninth steps of initiation (Poole n.d.: 54). The fat is from the wild male boar, which according to Poole represents semen. This is a stark contrast to Baktaman conceptions: though wild male boar is an enigmatic symbol for them (Barth 1975: 201f.), it is above all the embodiment of vigour and virility as an *opponent*, as the great despoiler of taro gardens and categorically opposed to the forces of fertility and increase. Domestic pigs' fat, on the other hand, (only sows are kept beyond the piglet stage, and domestic stock thus depends on wild boar for impregnation) represents the anointing blessing of ancestors in various initiatory contexts associated with increase and growth.

Among the Telefolmin, on the other hand, this emphatically 'male' red paint of both Baktaman and Bimin-Kuskusmin is secretly associated with menstrual blood (the secret name for red ochre, cf. Jorgensen 1982: 10) and menstrual blood from a currently menstruating woman is even added to the concoction (*ibid.*)[2] Any such admixture among the Baktaman would be completely destructive to the integrity and good-sacred properties of cult equipment and activities; while among the Bimin-Kuskusmin it would appear to be 'ungram-

[2] Whereas the Tifalmin, an easy day's walk from the Telefolmin, make the secret equation of red and pandanus and male sexual secretions, cf. Wheatcroft, 1976.

4

matical', as menstrual blood is characteristically represented by black rather than red colour.

It is no doubt necessary to be somewhat attuned to these cults and symbols to realize the full impact of contrast and shock that such differences generate. Clearly, in a certain sense the symbolic objects and acts that I have picked out here are of a kind, though opposite; but they also enter so deeply into an elaborate set of connected meanings and ritual statements as to dramatically explode and destroy this common base. If one were to imagine a Christian from one English village who entered the church of a community some miles away and found an image of the devil on the crucifix, and the altar wine being used for baptism, this seems the closest analogy I can construct. But by no means do all the contrasts have this stark character of inversion. In other cases, sacred symbols explicitly elaborated by some Mountain Ok communities are left entirely tacit or unelaborated by others.

Thus for example *fire*. This serves the Baktaman as the vehicle for sacrifice, and there seems to be a certain awareness among them of an imagery of analogy between sacrificial smoke in the temples and the smoke of the swiddens in the gardens – but otherwise fire is not developed as a ritual idiom. The making of fire is a male prerogative, and a secret formula to promote its making refers to the small marsupial mouse *ubir*; but *ubir* does not figure among the large set of marsupials hedged by taboos and employed for secret sacrifices on various levels of sacredness.

From the Tifalmin, by contrast, Wheatcroft (1976) provides an elaborate description of the place of firemaking in third degree initiation, associated with male maturity and virility (corresponding to the *Mafomnang* mentioned above). At a stage in the proceedings, fire is made on the chest of the novice, using the nest of the small *wabil* marsupial (presumably cognate with the Baktaman's *ubir*). This fire-making act is mythologically associated with the Afek creator-mother myth, which constitutes the core of cosmological beliefs among most of the Mountain Ok communities (but not among the Baktaman). But other associations are also indicated: the senior who rubs the fire-making equipment is having *his* buttocks rubbed by another senior man with the wing of the fruit-bat (another multi-valent animal symbol, both among Tifalmin and Baktaman), while the congregated seniors sing: 'Oh sacred fruitbat penis: it comes and goes!' until, at the culminating moment as fire is created, they break out in: 'through the buttocks, the glowing tinder lights; oh fire!'

Finally, even the major modes in which religious and cosmological ideas are expressed differ between Mountain Ok communities. Among the Baktaman, hardly any myths are told or known, and a rich flow of multi-vocal non-verbal expression is only minimally accompanied by short cryptic verbal statements and songs, and hardly ever given even the most rudimentary verbal exegesis. Among the Mianmin – peripheral Mountain Ok on the north slope of the cordillera – a greater corpus of myths is found (Gardner 1983: 352), but they are

5

not central to the religious events, which involve essentially the revelation of ancestral relics, the utterance of secret names, and the singing of sacred songs. The Bimin-Kuskusmin, on the other hand, maintain an enormous corpus of secret myths organized in elaborate cycles, which are told as central parts of cult and initiation rites, and are also regularly commented, in appropriately secluded settings, in extensive verbal exegesis.

Let this serve as a provisional sample of the ethnography, and the kinds of local variation which it provides. How should an anthropological description and analysis of such a complex field best proceed? In contrast to Frazer's day, it is now an anthropological commonplace that the different beliefs and practices found in a culture are closely connected as a system, and that both their description and their meaningful interpretation must proceed with reference to this context and in terms of these connections. So the anthropologist gives a close description of the elements in the culture of a group, and through analysis constructs an account which reveals how the bits fit together. Alternative contemporary recipes for the present case would have to be: (1) Stick to one place only, and give a consistent and orderly account of the interconnectedness of all the bits in that one jigsaw-puzzle. (2) Make a series of functional or logical models for a range of different communities within a larger, delimited area, and work out a classification or typology for the systems found within that area. Or, perhaps most challenging, try with Lévi-Strauss to (3) construct a single model which, by inversion, transposition, and other logical transformations, can generate as many as possible of these forms.

The criterion of success in all three alternatives depends on how much *order* one can discover in the data and depict as logical consistency in one's account. Now this criterion is not as silly as it may sound – it is not that the question of degree of order in cultural phenomena is not recognized as a possible empirical question by modern social anthropologists. But by what available methods might one investigate the degree of disorder, and document its extent, in such a way as not to expose the author of the analysis to accusations of incompleteness of material and failure of adequate analysis? The issue is appositely illustrated by the correspondence in *Man* following Ron Brunton's courageous article 'Misconstrued order in Melanesian Religion' (Brunton 1980a). Though the discussion focussed on materials from a group unrelated to the Ok it is directly relevant to our concerns here. The discussion led essentially to the formulation of two positions and one set of misgivings.

(1) The orderedness of the material is far greater than anthropologists are wont to believe. It is for us to assemble all the bits presented piecemeal by the chance sequence of events and the incomplete confidences of the informed natives. Secret myths provide the key to explanation, and will, if the ethnographic endeavour is successful, reveal the logical completeness and unity of a secret and sacred world view (Juillerat, 1980: 732ff).

6

(2) A true reading of ritual depends, not on ferreting out the secret native explanation, but on showing how the rites reflect the constitution of the local social universe: its groups and statuses, and their relations. It is for us to represent these two aspects of native life so that their isomorphy is revealed (Gell, 1980: 735ff).

(3) The third, non-position, could marshall important insights and objections to both preceding positions; but it did not seem able to articulate a theoretical position that provided a coherent alternative viewpoint (Jorgensen, 1981; Johnson, 1981; Brunton, 1980b).

How do these viewpoints stand up, and how might they serve us for our present purposes? To Juillerat and the exegetical school, one might first object that to show that myth and rite say the same thing hardly resolves the old debate regarding the priority of the two (cf. Leach 1954: 13f) or indeed that they should not both find their source and explanation in some unidentified third factor. And more specifically to the present material: it is true that in a secret tradition it takes good personal rapport and much thoughtful questioning and reflection to avoid the deceptions whereby the integrity of secrets are defended, so the anthropologist is told authentic myths. The poverty or disorder of such data in the notebooks of any anthropologist is thus a very weak indicator of the degree of elaboration and orderedness of myths in the sacred lore of a community. But as I have tried to show in my Baktaman study (Barth 1975; esp. 217ff), the sacralizing import of secrecy in these traditions also has a profound effect on the epistemology of native thought. The *force* of the rites, as mysteries, depends precisely on how the practice of secrecy moves every form of absolute truth out of reach and places the congregation in a relation to the vital and awe-ful category of the unknowable as the essence of mystery. It is surely a very naïve and literal rendering of such a tradition to regard the least widely known version of each myth as the truest! (cf. Jorgensen 1981).

To Gell and the Durkheimian school which sees ritual as a reflection of society: it is surely unsatisfactory to argue purely from the isomorphy between (certain features of) rites and (certain features of) society, without regard to what local people may say. Their interpretations are not just a (questionable) source of *ad hoc* sociological ideas; they are in a constitutive sense 'what their rites say'. I am not arguing that the significance of rites is exhausted by regarding them as communication only (cf. Lewis 1980: 16ff), and even less that 'an informed native's' verbalized account of their purported content is compelling (Barth 1975: 228). But I am arguing that the cognitions and emotions communicated through rites are a very significant component of their meaning – to wit in this particular material, that Baktaman and other Mountain Ok rites are ways of grappling with understanding pandanus, marsupials, fertility and cosmos, and not merely reflexes of society – and so must be analysed for the tradition of knowledge which they sustain.

7

Secondly, and analogous to my critique of the exegetial school, I see no compelling argument for reading isomorphy as a causal link *from* society *to* the form of rites – a point to which I shall return below, chapter 8. And most strikingly, in both viewpoints I see the same weakness that explanation is linked with the premise of an encompassing logical order. Once this premise has been adopted, local variation becomes essentially uninteresting – it serves at best to expand the field of myths in which one searches for 'the' key, or it adds further isomorphies without illuminating those already found any more profoundly. But most crippling of all, these viewpoints entail that local variation must be reduced and controlled by delimiting the object of study. The analytical argument in both the exegetical and Durkheimian school depends for its force on isolating the object of analysis as a closed system, and making all of its parts fit, like the jigsaw puzzle. How could we hope to make such methods and templates serve us in the task of analysing and understanding the jungle of variation that you have glimpsed from my brief illustrations of a few features of Mountain Ok beliefs and practices? And indeed, how could we hope to capture essential insights in any tradition of knowledge and any extant society by imposing the patently untrue assumption of closure as our methodological premise?

The example of Lévi-Strauss, when he ranges over continents in his parallels and inversions of myths (Lévi-Strauss 1966b), might seem more appropriate for our purposes. But I cannot accept the ontological basis on which he pursues such far-flung comparisons. I feel intuitively committed to an ideal of naturalism in the analytical operations I perform: that they should model or mirror significant, identifiable processes that can be shown to take place among the phenomena they seek to depict (Barth 1966:v). What this entails is an admonishment that we must always struggle to *get our ontological assumptions right*: to ascribe to our object of study only those properties and capabilities that we have reasonable ground to believe it to possess. On this particular issue, that means we should be able to show that the cultural materials we connect by operations of transformation could indeed be thus related in their historical genesis, and that the operations of transformation we perform are indeed modelled from empirical events. Lévi-Strauss's methodology provides us with no guidelines in this respect.

In the case of Ok ritual material, however, I feel I have good reason to represent the traditions of distinct communities as genetically and historically connected and somehow transformable into one another: At the big rituals and initiations throughout the area, it is common for delegations of senior ritual experts, and frequently for novices from other groups, to arrive from considerable distances to be present. Thus a network of participation connects all centres and all major events throughout the area. Visitors are certainly sometimes deeply surprised and shocked at what they see in the occult performances they may attend in strange and distant places. Thus, for example, a Baktaman who had once attended a major Bimin-Kuskusmin rite seemed still, long after, highly ambivalent, and afraid and unwilling to discuss the matter at all. Yet, even such shock and fear is, in the Ok ambience, a suggestive religious experience; and the rituals of other neighbours, more frequently visited, will generally be more compatible and apposite to a villager's local imagery and interests. Thus, there is an undeniable sharing of a wider stock of ideas than those embodied in the rites of one's own community, and a potential whereby cultural materials can be, and clearly sometimes are, passed on to other communities and adopted or transformed by them. This provides the rationale for studying the many local traditions under a unified perspective – but to do so, we need to construct that perspective. This means identifying the empirical processes whereby the cultural materials in question are produced and transformed. For this purpose it is not enough merely to appeal to the theoretical construct of *bricolage* (Lévi-Strauss 1966 a): we must also provide the empirical evidence of what is in fact the process whereby cultural expression is constructed in the particular societies and domains we are treating.

What is more, the models on which Lévi-Strauss's exemplary logical operations and transformations are performed are all highly abstracted and rather limited in scope. I see no way to model the features of both ritual expression and social organization in the various Ok communities with sufficient complexity to retain the empirical features that interest me, yet give the models the required simplicity and closure to allow for the operations of transformation that are the essence of a Lévi-Straussian analysis. The adoption of his procedure would thus force us to interpret and represent Ok thought and life in categories so far removed from their own conceptualizations as to entail an extreme loss of naturalism also in our very account of these cultural facts.

My own previous analysis of Baktaman ritual, now strengthened in my view by the accounts provided by other anthropologists analysing cognate traditions, focussed on an attempt to discover the meaningful structures, and the message content, of the rituals practised among them. A critical study of these materials forced me to recognize that Ok ritual is primarily cast in an analogic code, rather than the digital codes exemplified by computer languages and assumed by most structuralist analyses of natural languages, myths, and rituals. Though it has been fairly widely recognized that ritual builds on metaphor (in the more conventional sense of e.g. Ricoeur 1978 rather than the highly abstract Lévi-Straussian sense of metaphor vs. metonym), anthropologists have been very reluctant to draw the analytical conclusions that must follow from this view. For an extensive discussion of these issues, however, I must refer to my Baktaman monograph (Barth 1975).

2

An attempt at systematic comparison: descent and ideas of conception

Since I thus reject the three procedures that I find characteristic of contemporary social anthropological treatment of problems such as those raised by Ok ritual and cosmological variation, I am forced to proceed more patiently and construct my own methodology through a stepwise, tentative description and analysis. For this, we need some kind of systematic procedure for representing the forms, and ordering them in relation to each other with respect to morphological features: we need a comparative methodology. It is a striking fact that, great as the emphasis has always been in anthropology on presenting our discipline as comparative, there is no established procedure which could be named 'the comparative method' (cf. Kuper 1983: 197ff). Comparative exercises have been pursued from very different premises and with very different purposes in mind. A range of descriptions may be laid out to build a taxonomy; the presence/absence of features may be mapped to depict distributions, often as a basis for constructing a quasi-history of cultural diffusion based on the age-area hypothesis; or a few cases may be idiosyncratically selected and compared, to illustrate structural contrasts or similarities.

Nadel's discussion of co-variation (Nadel 1951: 229ff) comes closest to defining a procedurally clear and rigorous methodology. Let us try to apply it to our present case. Nadel sees the comparative study of variation as the essential tool for anthropological analysis. Without reducing the emphasis on the holistic or systemic *description* of cultures and societies, he argues for the comparative testing of propositions stating necessary interconnectedness between *certain features* of such systems. He rejects, moreover, a *ceteris paribus* clause. Indeed, to arrive at valid generalizations regarding the causal or reciprocal determination of forms evidenced by systematic co-variation, Nadel stresses that the other features of society which do not enter into propositions of co-variation should specifically *not* be equal. Otherwise, the correlations depicted as co-variation may simply reflect some other, unrevealed, factor in these surrounding features.[1] Nadel's methodology should thus equip us to test

---

[1] It should be noted, from Nadel's own illustrations, that he is not concerned to establish mere correlation between particular 'traits', but connections between major institutions: age set organization, clan segmentation, and warfare; residence rules and joking relations; etc.

10

Descent and conception

the order underlying surface patterns, to identify the nature and extent of necessary order. By observing variation, we would be attempting to put strain on the order we claim to exist: if particular interconnections are indeed necessary, they should show stability or systematic co-variation in varying contexts. We may thus, provisionally, continue to formulate our problem as that of discovering the empirical extent of order, and its underlying forces, through comparisons of variations between the different Ok communities.

Firstly, I shall try to pursue a program of linking differences in religion with differences in social organization. I have already exemplified some kinds of variations found in religious systems, i.e. some differences in ritual observances, cosmological ideas, and the role of myth. Let me now try to sketch some major differences in social organization.

Along the southward-facing slope of the cordillera, these can be roughly ordered on an east to west axis. Basically, descent is reckoned patrilineally in the east, bilaterally in the west. The Baktaman and their close neighbours, including Bimin-Kuskusmin, have exogamous patrilineal clans; Faiwolmin further west (e.g. Imigabip) are grouped in agamous patrilineal clans, while the westernmost groups form predominantly endogamous kindreds.[2] Telefolmin and Tifalmin on the northern side of the divide are likewise bilaterally organized. Beyond them, further west in the Star Mountains of West Irian, (agamous) patrilineal clans reappear (Pouwer 1964).

The primary political unit among the Baktaman and their close neighbours is a territorial unit occupied by a largely endogamous multiclan community of c. 200 persons, grouped in a main village and some scattered hamlets. The Bimin-Kuskusmin, on the other hand, form one large political unit of c. 1000 inhabitants with a far more complex organization. Clans are distinguished as natal, associated, and captive; and the dominant population of natal and associated clans is organized into the two exogamous moieties of Bimin and Kuskusmin, each under the ritual leadership of one of the natal clans, the Watiianmin and Imoranmin respectively (Poole 1976, 1982). Western communities, on the other hand, are composed of one or a few predominantly endogamous kindreds. Thus nearly the whole population of the village of Migalsimbip is counted as members of the Yamkal (bilateral) descent group, whereas the population of Wangbin (population: 84), until recently divided into four kindred groups, decided they were too few to sustain these divisions and under the chairmanship of the patrol officer realigned into two kindred groups, named Fungayun and Wanengsayeun. In case of marriages between persons of different kindred groups, the child tends to be affiliated to that of the father. For political purposes, furthermore, these local villages and hamlets in the west are grouped into larger alignments of considerable stability, constituting the 'tribes' of Wopkaimin, Tifalmin etc. embracing populations of the order of 600–800 persons.

[2] But again, among a few foothills group in the extreme southeast, patrilineal clans are absent. For a more complete, though preliminary, survey of many of these variations, see Barth, 1971.

11

Cosmologies in the making

The organization of groups and steps in initiation likewise shows great variation. Among the Baktaman, age sets are formed about every ten years by the entry of a cohort of boys into first degree initiation; and from then on the whole set moves up through a ladder of seven steps, as a cohering group, each step in a set order, over an unmeasured time period amounting in practice to 15–20 years. All men must be initiated.

Among the Bimin-Kuskusmin, attemps are made to order the age sets into a cycle of four named, recurring age grades composed of succeeding generations. Persons who in terms of biological age become too anomalous in such pattern are apparently not initiated at all; males of the captive clans are likewise not initiated. The remainder form a cohort which passes through ten steps of initiation over a period of 15–20 years. Within this cohort, however, about one third of the novices are selected to undergo more esoteric, intensive training. Though the whole set passes through the same steps at the same time, this core or elite group thus obtains a more complete and profound understanding of the secrets; and future ritual specialists and leaders will be selected among them only.

Among the Wopkaimin in the west, on the other hand, initiations are regarded as consisting of basically three steps, though phases of the first step can be equated with separate stages of initiation among more easternly groups. This first step is done within the local community and represents the necessary entry into the system. The higher, second and third levels are performed in regional cult-house centres; their order can be reversed, and participation depends on the individual decision of the novice and his guardian. In Telefolmin and Tifalmin, there was a (now discontinued) more complex series of steps of initiation; these took place in a sub-regional and regional hierarchy of temples of which that in Telefolip, supposedly founded by the creator/ ancestral mother Afek, was the highest. Ritual experts from a number of surrounding tribes congregated for the most important events in Telefolip. As among the Western groups, the sequence of the highest initiations among the Telefolmin was somewhat variable, and they lacked the collective features of the age-set organization among the Eastern groups, allowing participation on an individual basis.

In a search for co-variation between such features of social organization, and the variants of Ok cosmological and ritual ideas, where would one start to look for connections? It is often the case when the method of correlation is employed, that few leads are developed as to what the significant interconnections are in the course of marshalling data for the comparison. The most fruitful discovery procedure in social anthropology is achieved if one pursues one's major hypotheses in the description itself, penetrating ever deeper into the implications of the connections that one is positing. The design of a correlation argument, on the contrary, is best realized by providing two or more independent descriptions and *then* pointing to the correlations embedded in those descriptions. One is then forced to leave the crucial hypotheses undeveloped and simple till the description has been completed; methodological attention focusses on a contrived operation of falsification rather than the generation of informed and fertile hypotheses. So also with Nadel's procedure for analysing co-variation, when employed in a study of institutionalized forms as I have set it up here (but see below, p. 10fn.). We are so to speak left adrift, free to choose any plausible hypothesis we might wish that connects a set of religious or cosmological ideas with a set of organizational features. Let us, for example, try to explore the connection between theories of conception, and the organization of descent, in this fashion, to see its force as a method for uncovering a deeper structure of connection and order behind the bewildering surface variations.

The common Baktaman theory of conception, also shared among their closer neighbours, is simple and explicit (Barth 1975: 77). The child springs from male semen as from a seed; it grows in its mother's belly as the plant grows in the soil; it is nourished from her blood, which is why menstruation stops with pregnancy. The identity of the child is thus completely determined by that of its father; the child shares the substance of members of its patrilineal clan, and this identity cannot be socially changed by adoption, filiation to the mother's clan, or any other arrangement. All members of a clan, no matter how dispersed and long separated, share this substance; and it should be noted that clans were separately constituted by emerging each from their separate karst hole and thus are entirely unrelated to each other in substance. Alternatively, a myth describing the origin of human life, society, and the compact between the living and the ancestors, has the large gray phalanger *Kwemnok*, whose secret name is *Awarek*, i.e. grandfather/ancestor, divide humanity into clans as they emerged from the ground, thereby establishing the covenant which is the basis for the blessing of taro fertility (*ibid.* pp. 83f., 93).

The shared substance between members of a clan is generally conceptualized as blood, but this is the living blood in one's arteries and is thought of as categorically distinct from menstrual blood, so no ambiguity arises. With respect to nourishing the foetus, on the other hand, it is also commonly claimed that repeated acts of intercourse are necessary to cause birth because the foetus also requires the nourishment of male semen until it has grown large enough so the quickening of life can be felt – after which intercourse should be discontinued.

We thus see a very clear charter or justification in cosmology for a social organization based on patrilineal descent. Why such descent groups should be exogamous, on the other hand, receives a less clear imprimatur. The standard justification for clan exogamy is that intercourse between clan members would destroy the fertility of the taro gardens if any fluids from such intercourse were to fall on the ground, and this is almost impossible to avoid. Only a much feared sorcerer in the neighbouring group to the Baktaman was scandalously reported to have cohabited with his sister, and without such dire consequences. This would indicate that the ban on intercourse within the clan is a moral rather than a magical injunction: neither the Baktaman nor their neighbours can be held morally responsible for a person they condemn, and have indeed evicted from the community (cf. *ibid.* p. 133), and so their taro has not suffered. Indeed, the people of Bolovip who hold the same ideas, are quite familiar with the fact that their neighbours to the west do not observe clan exogamy, and explain this explicitly by reference to the presumably different covenant which *those* have with *their* ancestors, resulting in this difference as well as other differences in cult practices. But also within Bolovip, two cohabiting couples have broken the rule of clan exogamy after the advent of external administration, despite great indignation and threats when they married. With characteristic pragmatism, objections quieted down after a few years when taro fertility proved not to be impaired, and the villagers now acquiesce to these two marriages, without however changing the basic rule or theory.

Moving to the opposite pole, the bilateral descent organization among the Telefolmin, a simple pattern of co-variation seems to be revealed. The Telefolmin formulate a theory of conception whereby the child is created from a fusion of male and female sexual secretions. More than one act of intercourse is needed to introduce sufficient paternal substance to build a foetus; but intercourse should be discontinued as soon as life has been created to prevent twins from being formed. The balanced, bilateral mixture of substances which compose the child thus corresponds closely to the bilaterality of the sociological descent organization. We seem, in other words, to be on the track of a method by which we might hope to find systematic interrelations, and the underlying order, in the broad field of variations represented by the Ok.

But the main source of Telefolmin ethnography, Dan Jorgensen, in a very elegant paper (Jorgensen 1982), anticipates parts of the argument I am here pursuing, and shows how gender relations and variations in culture between genders add complexity to this initially simple picture. The theory of conception given so far is that presented by men. Women among the Telefolmin argue that it is incomplete and describes the formation of the child's flesh and blood only. Bones, on the other hand, are created entirely from the mother's menstrual blood. In view of the place of ancestral bones as sacra in the secret, exclusively male cult, this is obviously a very significant claim. Jorgensen relates it on the one hand to a wider symbolic theme in life and cult of transformations between the forces/colours red (blood, earth, and see above for ritual contexts of red) and white (taro, shell valuables, bones) which lends it particular power and importance in Telefolmin thought. On the other hand, it clearly addresses the asymmetries between men and women in terms of power, secrecy, and control of (sacred versus natural) fertility: it is a strong move in the battle of the sexes. Thus *both* theories of conception are of ideological significance for the organization of society, not only for the system of descent

14

but also for other aspects of relations. The images of 'a society' and 'a culture' as units of comparison are dissolved; there is scope for attention to co-variation within as well as between such units.

The issues are further complicated when we extend the comparison to a third case: the patrilineally organized Bimin-Kuskusmin. According to their ethnographer Poole (1976, 1982), they subscribe to a tortuously complex theory of procreation (best known to men, but also to female ritual elders) which resolve the various themes of bilateral transmission, agnatic blood, and female life-force. Through repeated acts of intercourse, the father introduces semen which combines with a gelatinous mass deep in the uterus composed of the mother's fertile fluids, menstrual blood and agnatic blood. Yet further increments of semen may favour the creation of a male child, but are so severely depleting for the genitor as to not be recommended. Every person contains the agnatic blood of his or her Father, Mother, Father's mother, Mother's mother, Father's father's mother, Father's mother's mother, Mother's father's mother, and Mother's mother's mother. The four latter categories of agnatic blood are not passed on to descendants, but define the limits of the person's own exogamous kindred group. The semen of the father is infused with the agnatic blood of all the four lines first mentioned, and the whitish clot in the mother's uterus contains four lines of agnatic blood from her. These unite; and the various components of this combined mass each contain the essence from which specific parts of the foetus and child will develop. However, it is in the nature of agnatic blood that its activity is weakened by transmission through women, and only survives for three generations after such transmission. Thus the agnatic blood that passes in pure patriline is ascendant, and unalterably determines the child's lineage and clan membership.[3] The remaining parts of a child's anatomy are created from the distinctive substances received from each parent, in a pattern where the soft parts which decompose quickly at death derive from the *female* contributions, while bony structure and essential sensory organs are made from the *male* contribution, as are both semen in sons and fertile fluids (but not menstrual blood) in daughters.

Compared to the Telefol women's version, this reversal of ascribing the hard parts of the body to paternal substances thus secures a male source for the sacra, and the imagery of multiple lines of agnatic blood, weakened except in pure male transmission, secures a patrilineal primary identity. But a battle for influence continues, charmingly conceptualized in terms of a carnal and a spiritual 'navel' (umbilicus and cranial suture – presumably the fontanelle – respectively), with accusations that mothers cover up the spiritual navel of babies with mud and clay to counteract paternal influences!

---

[3] Though it is apparently in certain circumstances believed to be influenced by the consumption of certain taro, pandanus nuts, meat, and fat associated with the ancestral spirit of another clan.

Cosmologies in the making

But why the elaborate mixing of various lines of agnatic blood (glossed as 'men's blood') by the Bimin-Kuskusmin (cf. Poole 1984: 197)? Though a charter for patrilineal descent is salvaged with the idea of weakening through maternal transmission, this construct has much less compelling, self-evident force than the Baktaman one. Why should male blood passed through a female live on for three whole generations, equally strong from mother's mother's mother and father's father's mother, and then suddenly be untransmittable even from father to son? Ok people make wide use of a concept of spirit/soul/ consciousness (Faiwol: *finik*, Bimin-Kuskusmin: *finiik*, Telefol: *sinik*). In Baktaman terms, people of one clan are related through sharing of spirit, it is passed on from father to child and is often personified in the ancestral spirit. Telefolmin, on the other hand, say they do not know where a person's spirit comes from; they emphasize instead how poorly developed and loosely connected it is in the infant (an idea shared by the Baktaman), and how it is an aspect of the person that develops only slowly (Jorgensen 1982: 5). The Bimin-Kuskusmin, like the Baktaman, speak of shared clan identity in terms of spirit and regard it as passed on from the father alone. But it seems to me that with their construct of multiple agnatic blood lines they are forced to distinguish between agnatic blood and spirit (the two are fused in Baktaman thought), lest each person be inhabited by a host of different clan spirits making war on each other, as spirits are prone to do. Likewise, while the Bimin-Kuskusmin plurality of agnatic blood lines answers some questions regarding forbidden degrees in marriage, it fails to explain the other distinctive feature of their marriage rules: their organization into exogamous moieties.

On this level of concreteness, therefore, it seems very difficult to subject the materials to a systematic comparison in a search for institutional co-variation. The things we would wish to compare are not of one piece in each of the communities of our comparisons; they are differently connected to different other aspects; they articulate with wider syndromes (I would need, for example, to go more deeply into colour symbolism; the other connotations of soft, perishable, hard, and durable; the conceptualization of death, and the spirit world; or with respect to social organization: village and polity endogamy and exogamy, etc. etc.). These major areas of religion and society would need to be covered, taking all the pieces into account, and compared in six to eight localities, to cover only one of many necessary foci for co-variation. I despair at the task, particularly without a theory to guide me as to what is sufficient order, what is a satisfactory degree of isomorphy?

And what is more, the kinds of connections that can be shown to obtain between forms of social organization and forms of cosmology are not sufficiently compelling; nor do they leave the things we are trying to correlate sufficiently separate. It seems that our descriptions – even the thumbnail sketches I have given here – expose a certain mutual fitness in things rather than a necessity, and they do so by weaving the phenomena together into an encompassing,

16

interpreted context rather than by leaving them identifiably separate but linked. In other words, the data we are handling do not seem to have the properties they must have, if this methodology of studying co-variation were to serve us. Yet, if we are driven into a position where every idea and every symbol must be seen in the context of all others, and all of social life, description becomes an unending task, and comparison a meaningless program. This was, surely, one of the main dilemmas facing Malinowski, preventing him from ever pursuing systematic comparisons.

In this impasse, structuralism offers the recognized counter-thrust to an ever thickening description. But we would have to abandon our present level of concreteness in our representations of Ok cosmology for the sake of facilitating such a structural analysis. In the fashion of much contemporary social anthropology, such descriptive detail could form a major part of the prose in our text; but we would have to transform it and construct highly abstract renderings of a few select features of it *before* we could perform any comparisons. Our models would be limited to represent only a few formal features so as to allow the various logical operations that could encompass the variation cast in this abstract form; and our anthropological interpretation of native thought would be cast in categories entirely different from *their* conceptualizations. Thus, our comparative analysis would only succeed by moving away from the complexity and reality of people's lives and thoughts.

3

The possible interrelations of sub-traditions: reading sequence from distribution

Let us look again at this brief account of theories of conception and modes of descent among three Ok groups. The positions described look more like an argument than like status quo in three logically and functionally integrated systems. Each and all of the statements may be read as competing views on what are the facts of life. As such, they would be connected, not as logical inversions of each other but as confused disagreements within a broad tradition of knowledge. They would relate to social arrangements, yes, but perhaps as imperfectly realized strivings and visions of what life could or should be like, or as more or less shallow justifications of conventions or claims, or as statements about what appeared self-evident in the life context. Again we are back to the question of what ontological premises are entailed in the different methodological procedures. Is what goes on in these Ok temples and outside them better understood with the Durkheimians as the enactment of sociological tableaus, or is it closer to the truth to see them as episodes in the communication of and search for knowledge? Is their inherent order essentially limited to the 'syntactic' features uncovered by a Lévi-Straussian analysis, or is much and rich texture composed of systematic relations of a 'semantic', or an interactional, character?

Let us look to ourselves in an attempt to get our ontology right. It is a widely held ideal, which I share, that anthropological theory should have the property of being ultimately self-reflexive, i.e. be as applicable to the culture and life in which we participate as to other cultures and other lives. Yet frequently, we find social anthropologists trying to construct accounts of other cultures seen as enactment, or syntax, only; but when they choose to speak of ourselves, i.e. the discipline of social anthropology, they do not employ these structuralist viewpoints. Thus for example, Sir Edmund Leach who has probably done more than anyone else to convince us of the power and validity of structural analysis: when he sets out to write about the kind of social anthropology he finds interesting, 'that meant looking at the subject from an egocentric and historical point of view' (Leach 1982: 7). So he traces different ideas, viewpoints, arguments of substance between past and present scholars, and he explores the paths and departures of social anthropology as an emerging (and

18

very inconsistent and confused) tradition of knowledge with no pre-set and over-arching order. Or look at another book by an anthropologist, called *Anthropology and Anthropologists – The Modern British School* (Kuper 1983), with again the same approach. I propose that we should work on the hypothesis that the ritual occasions of the Ok people are major occasions in the genesis of *their* tradition of knowledge, as significant in it as the major monographs, seminal articles, and innovative lectures are in ours. The distribution of symbols, ideas, meanings and world views among the Ok is a product of such events. As their anthropologist, I should like to write a book which might be called *Cosmology and Cosmologists – The Modern Ok School.*

With this as my program – how should I best go about the task? I tried initially to work on what we might call the variations in curricula. I took my own materials on sacred symbols and the corpus of knowledge as they appear in major ceremonies of initiation among the Baktaman, and listed them in a column. I then did the same for the cognate initiations in Bolovip – closely related but 30 km west and 13 years later. Doing this, initiation by initiation, I hoped to be able to identify major features in which the two sub-traditions differed substantively: how were they alike and where did they take different positions, emphasize different ideas, teach their novices other premises and other priorities? Then I added a third column for Imigabip, the next community to the west from Bolovip. My source on Imigabip was an interesting Ph.D. thesis by Barbara Jones (1980) – but one that focuses on illness and curing. It consequently proved very incomplete for my purposes, and interpreting those differences I found was difficult. Could the non-reporting of phenomena be read as empirical absences? Did obvious differences in emphasis reflect the effects of male secrecy on the work of a female anthropologist, or a greater access to female conceptualizations, or traditional differences between Imigabip and the other two communities? I then extracted a similar column on the Bimin-Kuskusmin from Poole: he devotes a five-volume, 2148-page thesis to their first degree initiation (Poole 1976). Yet even this account was not fully adequate for my purposes (as of course mine would not be for his). Besides being a measure of the remarkable wealth and productivity of Ok ritual, this clearly reveals unresolved problems in how such an analysis might be conducted.

But first: what precisely would be the purpose of such a comparative exercise? It needs to be recognized that my purpose, and therefore also my procedure, are different and more specific than the comparative methods more commonly exemplified in social anthropology. The exercise thus does not fall under any of the four headings discussed above (typology, diffusionism, structural contrasting, and co-variation, cf. p 10.) Rather, it seeks to identify the developments, departures, and dogmatisms of each of the small local centres *within* a tradition of knowledge, to discover the patterns of variation and thereby the underlying *processes* of thought, innovation and stimulus at work within it. To do so I would need to map out the local variation that has resulted from historical processes, in the form of a multi-dialect encyclopaedia of sacred symbols and concepts; then see this as a moment's cross-section of ongoing development; and hopefully to distil from it a historical account of current and recent shifts. The closest analogue which I hoped to emulate might be that of aligning vocabularies from different dialects and cognate languages so as to arrive at an inductive account of the regular sound shifts that have taken place in such a group of languages.

As I tried to work along these lines, the experience of insuperable difficulties of method and technique grew. An immediate one concerned the presence/ absence criterion for particular items. Dealing with these very complex and extended ritual occasions, one is hardly justified in regarding the non-reporting of any particular detail in an account as evidence of its absence in the rites described. Every account is necessarily abbreviated and concentrated, and different investigators will have different criteria for judging what needs to be included, depending both on their analytical theme and their idiosyncratic interests. Even when working with my own materials as represented by the totality of my notes and recollections, doubts arose. When some particular feature, e.g. in Poole's account of Bimin-Kuskusmin rites, appeared unfamiliar – could I feel sure that I would have noticed it, if it were found among the Baktaman in 1968?

Even when pondering my comparative columns from Baktaman and Bolovip, I became doubtful. For example, the second step of initiation among the Baktaman is called *Katiamban*, while an initiation of the same name and the same focus on showing the clan relics to the novices takes place in Bolovip as late as the sixth step of initiation. Being more senior and experienced, the novices in Bolovip's *Katiamban* are shown a much fuller account of the elements of clan sacra and cult, as one would reasonably expect. But are the same basic ingredients there in the shorter Baktaman version? My sources on these two initiations are limited to the verbal accounts of ritual seniors and novice participants (but I do not think direct observation would have resolved all the difficulties, since the contents of each rite is complex and many-layered). One episode or sequence in the Bolovip account describes how seniors collect the white *falong foon* flowers in the forest (if they find them). They then mash pre-dried *wanim* creeper[1] and a pitpit (*tarrung im*) which turns black when cooked, and mix them in a container made of the belly of a rat. This mixture is fed to the novices under the arc of a rat's tail, while they hold the white flowers in their hands, and a song making reference to the

---

[1] I believe this to be the same as the Baktaman *warengamnong* creeper, which commonly invades taro gardens and is used ritually, cf. Barth 1975: 84.

20

dinoghin bird (a black-and-white flycatcher?) is sung. I am confident that no trace of this rat theme appears in the Baktaman equivalent; and the use of the rat's tail to mimick the frequent use of a pig's tusk to sacralize the ritual food given to novices is a salient and highly significant inversion which I likewise did not find among Baktaman. But I am much less confident regarding the absence, in my notes, of any mention of white flowers, and white/black colour symbolism, in the Katiamban sequence among the Baktaman. Such elements may well be there, unmentioned or perhaps disguised, as one of the many secrets incorporated in the rite but kept hidden from the immature novices who are being 'shown' the Katiamban. In the case of most of the concrete symbols and acts, we are dealing with materials full of ambiguities, temporary deceptions, levels of secrecy, and cryptic hints that may be marginal, or terribly crucial, to what the organizers see as the deeper import of the rite. Perhaps even real absence, like silence, may sometimes speak more loudly than presence of the physical element to those who know the code. Thus, instead of being able to align fairly straightforward descriptive data in a first step to compare the component elements of a ritual found in two communities, it seemed necessary to judge the relative saliency of a range of underlying themes in a complex interpretation of whole ceremonies, or whole series of ceremonies.

Even when trying to stay closer to an account of each separate sacred symbol, difficulties arose. What is 'the meaning' of black, of rats, of a weed creeper in the taro gardens or the *dinoghin* bird, among the Baktaman and to the men of Bolovip? Through their manipulation in complex ritual, and their occurrences in daily life, each becomes associated with a fan of connotations, and split in a multiplicity of levels of ambiguity; and so each comparison becomes far too multidimensional and cumbersome in proportion to its significance.

Perhaps this is in the nature of ritual and secrecy, and needs to be recognized, not overcome, by our methodology. But it is also important that we do not give it wrong proportions, and depict the symbols and ceremonies as more bizarre than they really are in the perspective of human traditions of knowledge in general. I find it revealing to return briefly to my comparison with 'Anthropology and Anthropologists', hopefully without stretching the analogy too far. Let us imagine we were to give an account of the key concepts of social anthropology in the various local centres of the British School in the 1950s. To do justice to local refractions in Cambridge, Oxford, Manchester, the L.S.E. etc., of a few concepts such as 'lineage', 'Malinowski', 'matrililateral cross-cousin marriage' and 'fieldwork among Lapps' would require the explication of a considerable range of connotations and ambiguities of undeniable importance to the scholarly positions and visions at the time and their subsequent developments. Clearly, my aim to reveal the patterns of disagreements, variations and parallels in the local streams of a tradition of knowledge cannot be achieved by comparing columns of relatively straight 'descriptive' data.

21

Cosmologies in the making

Another general lesson from this attempt to interpret the variation as a result of historical developments is the repetition of the frequent and painful anthropological experience that a historical viewpoint holds no magic key where a reasonably sound and detailed historical account of the events of change is lacking. Even had I been able in my comparative tables to characterize and summarize the ideas and varying nuances of cosmology in Baktaman, Bolovip, Bimin-Kuskusmin, and four or six other communities at the various timeless moments when they were visited by fieldworkers, no vision of trends, sequences, or decisive events would have emerged. Granted, for example, that I could establish the 'rat theme' briefly noted above in the Bolovip Katiamban to be indeed unique for them – what would be the historical conclusions I could draw?

Let me sketch some context for the question. The taxon *sanok* refers to the zoological species domestic rat in Faiwol (though the word is also used as an alternative term for *kayuk*, the striped bandicoot). Such rats are widely regarded as unclean and disgusting among the Faiwolmin, and they are taboo to eat. When appearing as they do in the Katiamban of Bolovip, this suggests a series of enigmas and ideas. One or several senior women, renowned for their ability to raise good taro gardens, are sent out to kill the rat; it should be taken in a planted garden. Eating in a sacred context what is forbidden in profane life is a frequently employed way to point to a hidden significance for the object thus treated. Briefly, the appearance of the rat in this ritual episode links up with some widely distributed ideas among the Ok. Ok sacred knowledge gains much of its force from a dramatization of how the hidden significance of things is often the obverse of appearances, suggesting a mystery of transformation brought about by the blessing of ancestors. An individual experience is contrived whereby what was thought unclean and impure is revealed to be pure and sacred. This seems to provide a template for mystical transformations: what is unclean and impure can become clean and life-giving. Indeed the deepest mysteries of life and cosmos are precisely about such transformations. Thus destruction becomes creation: killing and harvesting destroy life, but also sustain it as its necessary prerequisites. In the growth of taro under the ground, dirt becomes food. By the heat from pre-heated stones, hard and unpalatable vegetables and meat are transformed to edible foods. Human sexuality and fertility can be represented as a parallel mystery, whereby the opposites of polluting women and female secretions, and men purified by their cult practices and taboos, unite in a carnal act and create spirit. While the male cults in the north and west make much of female sexual fertility in these terms, employing graphic idioms in the context of ritual, among the Baktaman the prototypical fertility mystery focusses on the dirt-to-taro transformation. The rat idiom allows Bolovip to associate women with the mystery of vegetative fertility, but without elevating female physiology to the role of the crucial, lifegiving force as is done in the deeper secrets of Telefolmin and Bimin-Kuskusmin. The

22

imagery of Bolovip associates women with the polluting and untransformed element in the mystery. It is they who bring the unclean rat that raids gardens and destroys taro; it is not their power but the power of male ancestors in the Taro House that transforms this impurity and destruction into growth and food, epitomized by the white flowers in the novices' hands – white being the colour of taro and plenty.

Even if these modulations of cosmological theories, and their synchronic distribution in Ok communities, were mapped in massive detail, however, they would not provide the kind of historical evidence we have been seeking. Not even the gross currents of contemporary thought in these traditions of knowledge can be read from such a map. Is Bolovip the last bastion of an old vision, which has been developed and elaborated in Telefolmin and discarded in Baktaman? Is it a recent and not very compelling attempt at a synthesis? Is it a first step in a change from a Baktaman-type view to a Telefolmin view or perhaps a step in the opposite direction? In this approach, we are trapped in reasoning that proceeds in the wrong direction: the answers to these questions should not come at best as highly tentative conclusions – they should be primary data, providing the premises for an understanding of just how these traditions of knowledge work, what their vital and inspiring ideas are. Yet, the historical/genetic viewpoint has a strength also. Looking at the various forms of rites and cosmologies as a product of (a complex, multi-causal, possibly in part fortuitous) history turns our attention away from constructing models of order and pattern in cultural manifestations, and towards the search for events that cause and shape these manifestations. It partitions the totality of the world differently for us: We can ask what ideas, experiences or conversations have *preceded* a certain statement and enabled it, as distinct from how the ideas and statements all exhibit a common pattern. Even when we recognize our failure to produce documented evidence of the broad sweep of history that has pro-duced these particular varieties of belief and lore: can we salvage some of this strength by marshalling other, more available, data?

4

The context for events of change

To do so, I must break out of the mold I have followed in the preceding chapter when setting up my problem and line of argument. I suggest that we here, as so often, can take a cue from Darwin. His strategy was to focus, in the tradition of the wondering naturalist, on small parts of the picture, closely observed and revealingly interpreted. He did not reach directly for the overall pattern in a myriad of forms, or the general shape and direction of phylogenies. Whether in the courting disply of golden pheasants (Darwin 1871: 728) or the relations of beak form, environment, and feeding habits of Galapagos finches (Darwin 1843: 373) he looked for generalizable features in the particular situation which might give cumulative direction to small increments of change. In other words, he sought to extract generalizable mechanisms and processes from his particulars.

Can we achieve something similar? Let me start with a scene from the temple in Bolovip. For a while during February 1982 I spent some hours every day there obtaining detailed descriptions of the rituals at each level of their nine-step initiation. Three persons participated from the Bolovip side: the former leader of the Yolam (the more recent leader had some days previously died in an accident during a sacred hunt), the senior man of the Katiam, and one other senior man. They were willing to speak with me about these secrets only because they knew, from independent sources, that I had passed through the initiations among the Baktaman. Apparently, the situation was defined by them as analogous to the discussions on local ritual customs sometimes pursued by senior experts from different communities in preparation for performances.

The Yolam leader had been the main informant, only occasionally supplemented by the others. The Katiam leader had been the most ambivalent, being visited in his dreams by ancestors who feared I would misuse what I was told. We had reached Mafom initiation (associated with pandanus wigs and red colour, the fifth step in Bolovip, equivalent to fourth among the Baktaman). On this day, the Katiam leader – at first reluctantly – took centre stage: he was the Bolovip specialist and organizer of Mafomnang. After some preliminary hedging he brought out a secret bundle and started unwrapping his equipment.

24

Events of change

From the grubby old piece of tapa he extracted the finger bone of an ancestor (for blessing, power and support), a spatula made from an eagle's longbone (for mixing the red ochre), the claw of a flying fox (for shredding pandanus leaves for the novices' wigs) – each a very dense and ambiguous symbol. These, he explained, had all been passed to him from his father, who had been senior Mafom initiator before him. He then proceeded with his detailed account of the ten-day main ritual, showing occasional (correct) comparative knowlege of the corresponding Baktaman rite and also of some other local variants (where I could not check the correctness of his account). The full contents of his Mafom bundle was, however, never exposed; and some parts of the ritual were also kept secret. The Yolam leader confirmed that parts were also unknown to him; he would be able to produce a Mafom initiation but only in its major outline and therefore with reduced or questionable efficacy. At no point did the description or ensuing conversation turn into an explanation or exegesis of the rite; it remained throughout a rendering of the initiation itself: its events, acts, and equipment.

What can we extract and try to generalize from this vignette? It is essential to remember that the rite is performed approximately once every ten years in Bolovip; until its next performance the initiator and other Bolovip seniors may have the opportunity, if they so choose, to attend at most 4–5 other variants of the corresponding rite in neighbouring communities. Meanwhile it is difficult for anyone to create and define the highly guarded, reluctant social situation in which the Mafomnang is discussed – rites are for doing, at the appropriate occasions, not for idly chatting about. Thus, the whole rite would appear to be lodged in one person's safekeeping, hedged by fearful taboos, represented by secret thoughts and a few cryptic concrete symbols during the long years of latency. When time comes around again, the leader of Mafomnang has the personal responsibility to recreate it, since there is a secret residue of its performance which he shares with no one. Other ritual experts form a critical audience, sharing many of the secrets but respecting the essential contribution of further secrets and thus the necessity to grant him collegiate recognition and trust, judging the performance above all pragmatically by its results. And these pragmatic tests are twofold: (i) a congregation of novices should be spellbound, transported by the mystical experience and emerge from it as changed men; and (ii) taro growth, other vegetable fertility, and the physical welfare and virility of the initiates should be enhanced.

This scene in the Bolovip temple thus represents one of the rare externalizations of Mafomnang between its even rarer manifestation in concrete performances. It shows us a particular individual in a recognized role as the guardian, on behalf of the collectivity, of a cultural entity of acclaimed great value, holding it in storage for reenactment a decade hence. As far as the cultural reproduction of Mafomnang and similar initiations, we seem to be faced with two possible extremes of interpretation. (i) Perhaps the form of the

25

rite is essentially figured in many other cultural products: in a range of sacred objects which serve as concrete symbols; in well-known myths; in other sacred or everyday sequences enacted frequently; in a repertoire of idioms constitutive of Bolovip culture; or even in a standard, memorized instruction or recipe for how to stage a Mafom. If so, to perform the infrequent Mafom one needs only to deduce its form from one or several of these accessible and extant sources. The emphasis on secrecy and the Mafom specialist's responsibility is, in this case, only a part of the mystifying social organization which enhances the cultural value of such initiations. (ii) Alternatively, major parts of the form of Mafomnang may be unique in this culture, so that its reproduction at the regular, rare occasions may be heavily dependent on what has been stored in the interval in one or a small number of minds: cherished, mystified and secret in the individual's keeping. I labour this difference because it makes an essential difference to the mechanisms of reproduction of these particular items of culture. To understand reproduction and historical change we need to understand the functional system which is undergoing reproduction and change – in this case, is the process one of collective retrieval from socially accessible sources, or one of recreation from elements lodged in one or a few individual minds?

Baktaman and Bolovip seniors are very clear on this: they hold the latter view. When the ritual leader of the Baktaman decided to perform the sixth degree initiation during my residence there in 1968, he had to set aside several days to try to remember and reconstruct in his mind just how it was to be performed. He turned to a few intimates for help and discussion (Barth 1975: 230), but they likewise saw the task as one of remembering, with the subsidiary question arising of whether they should copy the neighbouring community and adopt a new procedure for one of the parts of the ritual (*ibid.*: 91 f). Other evidence points in the same direction. Most senior men had only fragmentary recollections of even the elementary initiations through which they had passed. When I asked them for accounts of their own initiations, and interpreted their poor descriptions as evidence of reluctance to tell me, they defended themselves by stressing how it is this way for everyone: 'You know how it is during your initiations: your *finik* (spirit, consciousness) does not hear, you are afraid, you do not understand. Who can remember the acts and the words?' Without cultural ideas of rote memorizing and mnemonic devices (and of course without any notion of literacy) the Baktaman were likewise amazed at my ability, from taking notes, to recollect and learn the esoteric information I was given; so they quickly concluded that I must have extensive previous knowledge of secrets and so be already a ritual specialist in my own society. In other words: Baktaman do not seem able to deduce the forms of an initiation from other sources. A general command of Baktaman culture was in no sense thought to entail the foundations for knowing cult forms and procedures.

Events of change

Indeed, the Faiwol seem to live with the constant fear of loss of the vital knowledge. With the necessity, as they see it, of deception of the uninitiated, and the sacralizing power of secrecy (cf. Barth 1975: 170, 217ff.), the general idea among them is that transmission from elder to junior is in perpetual danger of being lost: 'This was all our ancestors told us.' In cases of recognized failure of transmission, however, the traditions of neighbouring groups are, under fortunate circumstances, available to replace the parts of one's own trandition that were lost.

Recreation of an initiation after the interval of about ten years since its last performance seems to depend in part on remembering that performance in detail, in part on remembering the instructions and secrets previously communicated by elders in rare and highly charged moments of revelation of sacred truths. It is difficult to ascertain the extent to which ritual elders themselves recognize the possibility of, or themselves practice, improvisation and guesswork, or conscious innovation, other than the above noted borrowing from neighbouring groups. The dogmatic view is certainly that all cult activities are based on a received tradition from ancestors. Nor was I able to identify any distinct concept of innovation at all, perhaps because the stepwise dramatic revelation of secrets through initiations dominates the individual experience and provides a template that conflates subjective novelty with objective innovation.

Do we have any way of discovering what happens to the cultural materials of any particular initiation, during the years while they are 'stored' by the senior adept and when they are again made manifest at its next performance: do innovations take place? I have argued at some length elsewhere that Faiwolmin religious cults persist by a variable balance between loss and accretion, and I have identified a certain number of recent historical innovations in the Baktaman rituals (Barth 1975: 239ff, 260). On this basis I identified some fields in regard to which there appeared to be evidence of creative, culture-building work being done within the Baktaman religious sub-tradition. These focussed on certain multivocal symbols which seemed unclearly conceived and articulated, and also on some symbols in terms of which relations and hierarchy between initiation sets were expressed (*ibid.*: 240ff). In the present context, however, we need to focus not on *where* in the total field of knowledge and ritual this creative work was taking place, but on the *mechanisms* involved in such creativity, or other kinds of modification, of cult and initiation forms. Our basic problem is to find the most fertile way to conceptualize the locus and mechanism of incremental change in this functional system composed of an organization of ritual specialists, sets of initiates, ladders of initiatory levels, and strata of cultural materials contained in these levels. If we can do so relatively successfully, we should be in a position to identify the major processes involved in generating diversity within the Ok religious tradition. This

27

will depend, in my view, on our ability to construct a schema of description and analysis with the required naturalism, or, as it has been phrased above, to get our ontology right.

How then might we best conceptualize what we see in the few concrete examples I have quoted? I do not think we can usefully borrow linguistic imagery of speech performance vs. rule, *parole* vs. *langue*. The staging of, for example, a particular Mafomnang does not build on an articulated set of often-applied rules, or a paradigm, as I have tried to show above. It is therefore necessary for us to avoid the linguistic models that build on the contrary assumption.

Likewise, and even more importantly, I wish to argue that we should be careful not to schematize the material too simply in a dichotomy of individual vs. collective. I have emphasized the aspect of cultural materials being stored for safekeeping in the mind of principally one single ritual expert in the long periods between their manifestations in performances. But dichotomizing individual and collective, person and society, easily invites an unnecessary separation of the data into two distinct universes, suitable for psychological and sociological explanations respectively. This separation may have been necessary, and was certainly productive, in Durkheim's time; but when it appears in anthropology today it tends to be associated with the assignment of far too much to the individual side of the dichotomy, and a failure to apply interactional and cultural insight to what is thus assigned. If we return briefly to the scene in the Bolovip temple which I sketched, it is nothing if it is not a moment in an enduring *relationship* of an individual to a collective. We are observing a person performing his role, making a statement which is an individual statement, but one shaped and authorized by a group, and required by the college of other ritual seniors who are his audience to be acceptably coherent, moving and compelling. Social science is now well equipped to describe and analyse such interaction and social process from the point of view of a single participant; it is no longer necessary for us to choose between distinct templates of either a society which is a whole and more than the sum of its parts, or an individual composed of an internal psychodynamics and a set of external stimuli. Further, when we must recognize that the ideas that compose the Mafom initiation are stored in a mind, we are recognizing nothing which is not a necessary part of every social act. Social science makes no sense at all unless we assume that every person's mind is full of representations of cultural objects, which are handled by mental processes and in due course give shape to the person's acts. Again, anthropologists – together with other social scientists and philosophers, besides psychologists – are certainly equipped to analyse many of these mental processes too, depicting them as deduction, evaluation, preference, strategy, etc. What is notable and important to depict insightfully in our description of the present case, is the sociological circumstance that it is

mainly located in *one* mind for long years, governed by the cultural impera-
tives that it should be held secret, cherished and mystified and then suddenly,
dramatically be made manifest.

Obeyesekere provides a very stimulating template for this kind of situation
in his study (1981) of Sri Lankan extatics. Working within a predominantly
psychoanalytic paradigm, he none the less provides a model of process in a
highly generalizable form. He is concerned with the connection between the
public meanings of cultural symbols, and their private motivations or uses as
personal symbols. Through detailed case studies of some individual extatics
and their religious experiences, he shows how public symbols can resonate
with deep personal significance, and thereby give identity and direction to
otherwise deeply troubled persons in roles and symbolic statements accept-
able to the larger society. Most appositely for our purpose, he discussed
subjectification as

the process whereby cultural patterns and symbol systems are put back into the melting
pot of consciousness and refashioned to create a culturally tolerated set of images that I
designated subjective imagery. Subjective imagery is often protoculture, or culture in
the making. While all forms of subjective imagery are innovative, not all of them end up
as culture, for the latter depends on the acceptance of the subjective imagery by the
group and its legitimation in terms of the larger culture (Obeyesekere 1981: 169f.).

On this basis, let us construct a simple model, or hypothesis, which may
assist us in identifying a mechanism of incremental change which can generate
a variety of rituals such as that found in the Ok religious tradition. We have
observed how the cultural content found in Ok cosmology is distributed between many sub-traditions located in numerous villages and temples, in intermittent and somewhat reluctant communication with each other. The cultural
materials that compose each such sub-tradition are further subject to a constant oscillation between public performance and solitary safekeeping in the
care of a small number of ritual experts. This would indicate that the integrity
and continuity of each sub-tradition depends on the successful recurrent
transformation of its constituent symbols as between a public phase and
modality, and a personal phase or modality. But there is every reason to
assume that each such transformation requires an active intellectual effort and
thus stimulates – no, indeed requires – creativity on the part of the ritual expert:
to re-create in the one modality materials articulated in the other. The results
of such creativity cannot be expected to produce complete identity of content,
but rather to entail potential for incremental modifications within each sub-
tradition, canalized but not controlled by the sanctions of each respective
audience.

The concept of subjectification in this oscillation gains particular force as a
model for what may happen in these transformations, when seen in connection
with my analysis of the basic structure of the ritual idiom in which the tradition
is cast (cf. Barth 1975 and chapter 10 below). This suggests that a close

homology obtains between the metaphoric/analogue structuring of the public symbolism, and primary process thinking. Whereas for example a logarithmic table, subject to the same oscillations, would be exposed to no creative elaboration and considerable danger of banal error, cultural imagery cast in the analogue code of metaphor is closely in tune with the mental processes of each individual ritual expert, and thus malleable by his creativity. Such cultural materials are indeed 'put back into the melting pot of consciousness' (see below, pp.71ff.). Moreover, the encapsulating, privatizing effects of secrecy will plausibly further loosen constraints on fantasy and elaboration in the ritual expert's relations to the materials in his keeping. But the most general point, and least controvertible, would merely affirm that the 'storage' in the individual mind, without literary aids, of complex cultural materials over long time, followed by a demand for their manifestation in complex and vital performances of mystery cults, must be highly evocative of personal involvement by the ritual expert in the cultural symbols in his keeping, and could be expected to result in his marginally reshaping them in form and content, in harmony with his own visions, at every new performance.

This model incorporates the self-reflexive properties for which I called in my comparison with our own accounts of contemporary social anthropology (p.18). I have argued that contemporary Ok cosmology is conceptualized primarily in concrete symbols and communicated through a variety of ritual performances of which initiations are the most infrequent but also the most important. I shall try to show that the form and contents of this tradition are shaped through the particular history of an intermittent conversation between ritual experts and their audiences – not by reconstructing that history, but by indicating how a model of the processes involved in that history can generate the particular range of empirical forms reported from the Ok region.

---

[1] I do not, of course, claim that these constructions have any basis in comparable Ok self-interpretations. Indeed, they pose questions on a meta-level in which I have no evidence that Ok thought has ever moved: to my knowledge Faiwolmin, and other Ok populations, are not concerned about the sociology of knowledge. It is for *our* project of a comparative anthropology of knowledge that I claim these models and interpretations to be illuminating and fertile.

5

The results of process – variations in connotation

My next task will be to show that the different idioms and ideas represented in the sub-traditions of Ok ritual can be related as possible transformations of one another. But here lies the crux of my analysis: I am not proposing to demonstrate merely that one pattern can be transformed into another by arbitrary operations of inversion, transposition, etc. I am working towards an identification of the main empirical mechanism of change in the material under analysis; and so I must demonstrate that a model representing this mechanism, operating over time, does indeed generate a variety and distribution like that obtaining among the Ok. Stated abstractly, the methodology requires that my rules of transformation must mirror empirical process, as this is represented in the model. Stated substantively, I am trying to marshall support for the hypothesis that it has been through the operation of repeated oscillations of cosmological lore between its private keeping and its public manifestation by responsible cosmologists in sequestered temples, that such modifications over time of Ok cosmological traditions have in fact taken place.

Thus, the key question is: what would be the sequences and directions of change, if my model of subjectification and re-objectification correctly depicts the main dynamo of creativity and innovation? Briefly (and I shall develop this argument through the next three chapters), I see three forms of change as plausible results of such a process: incremental shifts in the fan of connotations of sacred symbols; incremental changes in the saliency of various meta-levels of significance of sacred symbols; and incremental elaboration or reduction of the scope of particular logical schemata in the cosmology. Each of these shifts can take place, and can be expected to take place, as an unintended and unnoticed trend changing the real content of the lore transmitted in any particular temple, given the way these traditions of knowledge are organized, expressed and transmitted.

Do the features of contiguous sub-traditions of cosmology actually show the variations that would be generated by such changes? In the present chapter, I shall try to show that they do with respect to the first form of variation, in the fans of connotations of sacred symbols. The next two chapters will explore the other dimensions of variation, reflecting the other two trends of change.

Cosmologies in the making

I shall use *water* as my first example. The power of water as an agent of removal is widely recognized in Ok imagery. Water washes away dirt, erodes the land, streams carry away flotsam and debris. Telefolmin, Faiwolmin and others throw dead persons (hated enemies, sorcerers, etc.) into rivers to eliminate their spirits as well as their bodies; novices exposed to sacred influences but not yet assimilated to the higher sacred positions must not wash, or step into streams. Water in which you see the reflection of a bewitching spirit is thrown over the bewitched to remove the spirit. The basic cognition is thus focussed on transportation and removal, rather than laundering and purity as in Eurasian consciousness.

As a sacred symbol, water is highly significant among the Ok. For specified periods after all sacred performances, there is a taboo on drinking water; and a widely used term for persons who have completed one of the higher rituals is *kimitok*: '(allowed to) know/take water' rather in the sense of 'break-fast'. The water-drinking taboo is directly connected to the water's removing power by the Baktaman; abstaining from water conserves the sacred power which surrounds and penetrates persons in the ritual.[1] But over this theme, the Baktaman weave a paradox and mystery: water is hallowed as a secret symbol of increase and growth rather than removal and loss. The root metaphor is the miracle of dew: water which grows spontaneously on the leaves of the forest. Boys during first degree initiation among the Baktaman are taught to rub pig's fat on their face, to further growth; and this fat must never be removed with water. But on the very first night of their initiation the little boys are taken out into the forest where dew is forming, and taught to wet their hands with the dew and rub it on all parts of the body that have not been rubbed with pork fat. This is thought to mystically further their growth; and men continue every morning until maturity, and occasionally all through life, to rub themselves with dew in this fashion so as to promote their own growth and strength.

This can also serve as an example of one of the basic means by which Faiwolmin mystery cults are constructed. A substance or object with a widely recognized significance is revealed, to the select, to stand for some other and dramatically inverse quality, and to provide a metaphor for the transmission or conferment of this quality. The object thereby serves as a sacred symbol, and embodies an understanding of the real and hidden nature of things, which is different and sometimes the very opposite of what the ignorant and uninitiated believe. Such imagery is highly compatible with the mode of organization and communication of Faiwol cosmological knowledge: communication about cosmological matters takes place almost exclusively in the sacred, sequestered contexts of secret rituals and tabooed temples, and is largely cast in analogue,

[1] Indeed, fully initiated men escape some of the discomforts of the taboo by making the identification more precise: it is *running* water that removes – so if before a ceremony you collect a store of stagnant water trapped in leaf bases and natural hollows, this water can be drunk during rituals.

32

non-verbal codes. An aura of mystery and insight is created by dark hints that things are not what they appear. That ignorant assumptions are negated by guarded knowledge is the very stuff of mystery cult, and essential to the ritual expert in his role as the one who hides and reveals. At the same time, this provides a most suggestive and stimulating context for the ritual expert's own thoughts and fantasies while these cultural materials are 'in the melting-pot' of his consciousness during the long periods while they are *not* being revealed.

Back to water and dew. Among the Bimin-Kuskusmin, Poole reports a similar taboo on drinking during ceremonies; novices must not expose themselves to rain or step into streams; they must avoid plant and animal species associated with water; and there are occasions during the rituals when they must rub themselves with dew. But Poole reports a Bimin-Kuskusmin exegesis which links these observances to a pervasive hot/cold schema. When water must not be imbibed, it is because the sacred ritual is hot and water is cold; boys are made to rub and wash themselves with dew to 'cool' themselves after first contact with sacra (which, unknown to the novices, contain symbolic representations of the power of menstrual blood) (Poole, n.d.: 41f). Wild boar fat on the skin of initiators serves to insulate them against 'cold' winds.

Now the Baktaman are also familiar with hot/cold imagery, and heat provides them with a template for life force and sacred power, particularly in the forms of fire, the subterranean pit ovens in which taro for the great festivals are baked, and most especially in the sacred symbol of the Megapod bird, whose eggs are incubated by the heat generated in nest mounds of decaying vegetation (Barth 1975: 235f). But these idioms among Baktaman are linked in a syndrome of ideas into which water does not seem to enter significantly. Indeed, Baktaman effort is focussed on pressing all possible aspects of water into the removal vs. increase paradox: even rain is linked to this imagery through a rather elaborate contrivance. Thus, first degree novices are made to build elongated, miniature shelters c. 50 cm wide and 3–4 m long, covering a felled log. During their months of liminality when they sleep in leaf shelters in the forest they are made to get up at night every time strong rainshowers fall, rush to these shelters and lie down beside each other with their heads resting on the log – the little roof serving to shelter their fat-rubbed faces – while their bodies are exposed to the rain so as to receive the increase-power of the rain falling on their body, analogous to the way rain swells the ground and swells the streams (*ibid.*: 52, 54).

There can thus be little doubt that whereas water 'stands for' cold as opposed to hot in Bimin-Kuskusmin ritual, it is used to express the opposition of increase and removal among the Baktaman. While it might appear that 'coldness' is a much more basic and compelling significance for water as a symbolic idiom than is 'increase', the latter has the attraction of paradox, which thus makes it instrumental in furthering the 'mystery' aspect of the cult.

On the other hand, the function of water taboos in the Bimin-Kuskusmin cult is obviously not to comment on coldness, but to conjure up its opposite as immanent in the rites: to help express the presence of an abstract, mystical 'heat' that permeates the performance. Both messages are important in the cult context, and reasonably salient and inspiring. What we see, quite clearly, are different potentials of water as a concrete symbol being elaborated and used differently in the two sub-traditions.

Since Turner's seminal analyses, we have been familiar with multivocality as a regular feature of symbols, each having, as it were, a fan or spectrum of referents (Turner 1967: 50). There is thus no necessary contradiction between these two alternative imageries – indeed, both can be seen and probably are seen by the Ok in their existential context as inherent in water itself: water *is* cold in this mountain environment; it is truly inimical to heat in that it puts out fire; it does wash away substances; it does appear out of thin air as dew on leaves. Any one of these aspects of water could be used as an idiom in a particular context, without compromising or denying the other properties. But note how water as a sacred symbol is used for more than this: it is not a token for a particular meaning, but a vehicle for expressing a more complex and subtle message. The paradox of water as dew, as an imagery for the miracle of growth, is elusive to conception and resistant to communication. So is also the intangible presence of powers analogous to heat and fire, obliquely implied by there being something which is threatened by any trace of water. Experiencing and 'saying' these ideas by means of rites and concrete symbols requires personal effort and intellectual work, and the idea is clarified and transmitted better, the better the imagery is shaped as its vehicle. It is not productive of such clarity to use the idiom of water to express both these ideas at once.

The differences in how water imagery is used in Baktaman and Bimin-Kuskusmin ritual can best be understood as the precipitate of the work of particular ritual experts over time, transmitting and incrementally reshaping their respective, received sub-traditions. The idea, the conception, as it has impressed itself in the consciousness of the ritual expert, provides his blueprint of what shall be 'said'; his task is to retrieve the imagery that makes that idea immanent, and communicates it to novices. I think we can easily see how steps in a slowly emerging vision can lead from the properties inherent in water variously to the Baktaman and the Bimin-Kuskusmin message. Each oscillation between the public and private modality can constitute an incremental step in the vision's emergence within a sub-tradition that does not acknowledge that change and innovations ever take place, only that some performances come off better than others, that the eternal truths are sometimes more powerfully immanent and the novices sometimes more successfully transformed into knowing and seeing men than at other times.

It may be important at this point that I make explicit the epistemological status of these features of Ok ritual within the Ok tradition of knowledge. All the evidence indicates that alternative renderings, e.g. of 'water' as an idiom in ritual, are not just alternative vocabularies in which ritual messages may be expressed: they are themselves substantive cosmological statements. As such, the metaphors of Ok ritual should be read literally: the Baktaman are saying that the hidden, true world is so constituted that a power of increase is immanent in dew.[2] That which is embodied in Ok ritual struggles to be true knowledge, to build up a construction of statements about the true nature of significant objects and processes in the world, and the relations and forces that obtain between them (I shall return below, pp.66–73, to an attempt to refine this discussion).

In this struggle, the stepwise clarification of a concrete symbol does not necessarily lead to the definition of a simple significance as its dominant and authoritative meaning. On the contrary, the effort seems directed at constructing a harmonization of multiple connotations, i.e. an ordered multivocality, rather than merely suppressing many connotations in favour of the saliency of one. But this is not easily done, and in any particular Ok sub-tradition it is better achieved for some sacred symbols than for others. Let me illustrate this for the wild boar as a sacred symbol in Baktaman and Bimin-Kuskusmin ritual, mainly in connection with the pig's fat rubbing touched upon in the above material.

In my analysis of the Baktaman, I concluded that wild boar was poorly conceptualized in their ritual (Barth 1975: 250f). The beast is of consuming interest to them, and as a symbol it is important and highly multivocal; but its different connotations do not make good sense in relation to each other, and as a vehicle for constructive cosmological thought it is consequently unproductive. There are three aspects of the animal which dominate in Baktaman consciousness, epitomized by the male of the species. (1) It is man's enemy in a perpetual battle over the swiddens. Wild boar break down fences and ravage gardens, they are both aggressive and cunning, biding their time but grasping every opportunity. Wild boar is therefore seen as an anti-fertility force: as the great despoiler. (2) It is far the largest and also the most dangerous game animal, its meat is of high quality. It is therefore eagerly hunted – both for its meat and as a sign of the hunter's courage and skill. It thus stands as an embodiment of (enemy) strength. (3) Mountain Ok keep domestic pigs, but do not generally raise boars to maturity. Their sows therefore depend on wild boar for insemination: it is the essence of virility and male fertility.

Baktaman ritual codifications derive from the great despoiler theme and cast wild boar as the essential enemy, ritually as well as physically dangerous to garden and taro fertility. But little use is made of it as an idiom in formal ritual, except through the operation of tabooing it, and banning it from certain

---

[2] Obeyesekere interestingly cites his extatics who refer to their hypnomantic activities as 'research' (Obeyesekere 1981: 179f.).

temples. Bimin-Kuskusmin, on the other hand, use wild boar's fat in their initiation rituals as the essential symbol for semen; they inaugurate phases of their rituals by burning/exploding containers of such fat/semen, and they anoint their novices, and their taro plants in the sacred gardens, with it. Thus a creature of great inherent interest to members of the congregation is linked as a concrete symbol to the vast theme of man–taro equivalence and the male's fertilizing role in gardening and human growth.

If this is such powerful imagery, why has it not spread to the neighbouring Baktaman? Though the two populations have been fairly effectively separated by three days' march over very broken country, and mutual and third party enmity and insecurity, I know at least of one historical occasion when Baktaman novices have actually been incorporated in a Bimin-Kuskusmin initiation (around 1950); and the two populations are in regular contact through one intervening link. The idea of wild pork fat as semen must reasonably have offered itself to the Baktaman through diffusion; and, as shown by its Bimin-Kuskusmin elaborations, it could have served them to 'make sense' of wild boar in cosmological terms, and express ideas of the male role in taro garden fertility which are the very crux of much Baktaman ritual. If we were dealing with traditions that had the capacity for major, quantum leaps, I think it would indeed have been adopted; but idioms are embedded in systems of meaning in relation to each other, and in networks of ritual statements that are known, valued and moving. There is no obvious way in which the Bimin-Kuskusmin vision can be approached, through the incremental steps of change generated by subjectification, within the Baktaman sub-tradition.

Most significant here is the blockage set up by Baktaman conceptions of fat-rubbing. The fat with which novices are made to rub their faces comes from sacrificed domestic pigs, i.e. from materials left over from solemn occasions when fathers as senior initiates have reasserted their compact with ancestors through commensality with all senior initiates of the community, and with all the ancestors through fire-offerings to the exemplary ancestor of the Yolam temple. The young novices are still far from the point where they will be allowed to participate, or even to know of, these focal occasions; but meanwhile they are unknowingly being anointed in the deep sense of being consecrated, and receiving the blessing of growth from their ancestors when rubbing the fat on their faces. There is no way in which fat from the aggressive, powerful despoiler of gardens can serve this function; so as a vehicle for conceptions of virile fecundity the wild male boar becomes unexploitable, and as a sacred symbol in general it remains under-employed in Baktaman rites.

But this does not mean that Baktaman are not working conceptually with the beast, trying to make sense of it as a symbol. It is striking that of the nine recent attempts at ritual innovations I was able to discover among the Baktaman in 1968, three were concerned precisely with wild boar. One of them can serve to illustrate a potential direction of change, and a characteristic step of change generated by subjectification and re-objectification. I noted that wild boar among the Baktaman is taboo in the Yolam temple, the central communal temple for warfare and taro and most major rites. In the subsidiary Katiam temples, associated with clan cult, hunting and taro, on the other hand, wild boar is allowed together with all other forms of game that may be eaten by senior men, and figures among the trophies kept in such temples. Some time around 1955–60, 'the (c) set had just been initiated to 3rd degree; and as he emerged from that seclusion Ngaromnok came upon a very large wild boar in the act of copulating with a domestic sow. He shot it and killed it. When shortly later the (c) set, as novice warriors, joined their first raid they carried the mandible of this formidable animal with them in a net bag. The raid was successful, and Buryep, the cult-master at the time, thereupon incorporated the mandible among the *Yolam* sacra without changing the basic rule banning all other male boar meat or bones from the temple.' (Barth 1975: 241.)

It should be noted that third degree initiation is directly linked to warfare, but that the central temple in which the initiation takes place contains no trophies other than shields conquered in war – human bones are those of hallowed ancestors and animal bones those of domestic animals sacrificed at major ritual occasions. The act was thus a distinct departure. Its initiator, Ngaromnok, is a person of considerable intelligence and force. For a while as a boy, he had been lazy and was given a nickname equivalent to 'good-for-nothing'. This clearly stung him, and he decided to prove himself. He quickly married two women (plural marriage is a recognized act of bravado among the Ok, as also in some other parts of New Guinea), and he named his first child (who was one of the first children born to his initiation set cohort) 'Good-for-nothing' and insisted that he should be known by the teknonym Fibisal, 'Father-of-good-for-nothing', in challenge to those who had underestimated him so. In other words, we may see a number of features motivating a strong personal significance for the wild boar mandible as a private symbol. Ngaromnok was still in a very junior position to effect any ritual change, and that may be the reason why it was still remembered and acknowledged as such 15 years later. But the symbolism was cast in a culturally recognizable form, and became not only tolerated but adopted by his group – precisely, I would argue, because it addressed itself in an incremental step to conceptual problems which people could experience as unresolved. Continuing from this point, I can speculate on several developments of possible imagery – e.g. using wild boar fat, instead of certain sacrificial marsupials, to give power to the fighting and hunting arrows in the Wonsa ritual (*ibid.*: 70), and thereby opening for the identification of wild boar fat as symbolic semen. The essential point is that, within the context of existing ideas and expressions, such increments must add more sense than they subtract and confuse; they must lead along a meaningful track, if they are to effect any cumulative development of the sub-tradition. But the impetus arises in the melting-pot of a creative consciousness, doing the intellectual/fantasy work of re-fashioning images which in turn are used to conjure forth the sacred powers in the situation of public performance.

6

Secret thoughts and shared understandings

In the previous chapter I reasoned in terms of the actions of a single ritual leader's consciousness, working with culturally given materials and clarifying or harmonizing sets of implications and associations of the sacred symbols. When the products of such work are incorporated in public rituals and assimilated by the audiences, the result is an ordering and elaboration of the fans of connotations that characterize sacred symbols. In this way, the cosmological constructions of the different Ok sub-traditions are developed and elaborated in different directions. But there is also another aspect of the private use of symbols: when culturally validated and standardized symbols are used as vehicles for substituted themes and fantasies by the individual. If such themes and fantasies have a repressed or subconscious character, a disposition towards them may be widely present or easily induced, and thereby they may become shared in an audience or congregation through only mild suggestion and innuendo, perhaps largely unconscious both on the part of the person who originates the process and those who are influenced by it. Implicit and supressed metathemes can thus become established and developed, and thereupon be articulated and made explicit, till finally they become recognized as the essential themes of the ritual in question. This process is particularly facilitated by the secrecy of Ok cults, since the shared cloak of secrecy can take over many of the functions of internal repression, and the most sacred part of the message is generally thought to be the most hidden and implicit.

Particularly with reference to sexuality, one might expect such processes sometimes to operate. It is a striking fact that the various Ok cosmological sub-traditions show great diversity in emphases and degree of explicitness in their symbolic constructions over human sexuality, from the relative prudery of Baktaman, through suggestions of carnal lust and pleasure in Bolovip, and diverse and explicit emotional and physical imagery in Telefolmin and Tifalmin, to the riotous sexuality and androgyny of the Bimin-Kuskusmin. In the following, I shall try to summarize the relevant data briefly, to see if the process I have suggested provides a plausible mechanism, while reviewing the wide field of variation that results.

Starting, as I arbitrarily tend to do, with the position of the Baktaman, we see

38

Secret thoughts

a fairly limited and oblique use of sexual imagery and sexual templates in ritual. The generally resonant imagery is that of gender: as the congregation offers sacrifices of game caught during secret hunts to ancestors in return for taro fertility, their acts mirror those of husbands offering wives the game obtained through secular hunting, in return for the provision of taro corms from the gardens. The rites that most directly refer to human sexuality are those of Mafomnang, of which parts have already been described. Here we see the glory of male gender celebrated, in connection with the approximate time of sexual maturity of novices. There is particular emphasis on the presence of women and girls as audience to the novices' dancing, and on showing off the manly attractiveness of the handsome young novices, emphasized by the women who, uniquely in this initiation, congratulate each other with the beautiful appearance of their respective sons and brothers. Novices wear Bird-of-Paradise feathers for the first time – a bird justly famed for its courting displays – and during a four-day marathon dance they sing conventional love-songs as well as warsongs. But other references to sexuality are more figurative, such as the association of the red colour with which novices are painted with the red pandanus fruit – a very phallic image – and the attention to hair (on the head) in the elaborate braided hair-and-pandanus wigs.

The closely parallel Mafomnang initiation in Bolovip goes further in its specific reference to sex. Part of the procedure is to employ explicit elements of love magic. In preparation for the rites, one of the seniors collects mud from an unmarried girl's footprint which he dries over the fire and crumbles to a powder; this powder is mixed together with some feathers of the *wogher* bird (tentatively identifiable as *Monachella mulleriana*, a River Flycatcher), and from these elements he makes a bundle called *kisol morép* ('payment/token of desire'). The female *wogher* bird, it should not noted, can be seen along rivers and streams occasionally performing an almost indecently explicit tail-wagging ritual before its mate. When the novices are first collected in the forest, at the beginning of the initiation, the forehead of each is touched with this *kisol morép*; afterwards they are burned repeatedly with strong nettles. Later, when the festively painted and wig-wearing novices enter the village, the *kisol morép* is carried by the first of the line of novices and thrown on the first woman he meets. When describing these parts of the initiation, senior men were induced to a distinctly ribald mood. But neither in the Bolovip nor Baktaman material is there convincing evidence indicating that this sexuality is seen as connected with the main theme of ritual, as a model or a source for garden fertility or general fecundity and life force. Alerted by Poole's description of idioms in Bimin-Kuskusmin ritual, I note now with greater interest the injunction that Baktaman novices during the Mafom dance are allowed to eat taro rubbed or dripped with pig's fat, and no other food or water (Barth 1975: 74); but I have no evidence to indicate that this signifies, or is associated by the Baktaman with, ideas that the fat stands for semen fertilizing the taro.

39

Cosmologies in the making

The Tifalmin, as noted briefly (p.4fn.5), have an initiation closely parallel-ing the Mafomnang of the Faiwolmin, here appearing as the third of five steps and known as Selban, cognate to the *ser/sel* Faiwol term for the species of pandanus from which the wig is fashioned. Major parts of the rite are explicitly erotic, from the men's point of view. Some of the imagery used is vividly expressed in myth form: the creator-woman Afekan's handsome younger brother Towalok was so attractive to nubile young girls that Afekan became jealous and shot and wounded him with an arrow. Immediately, he was transformed into a male Bird-of-Paradise of one of the red species. As he flew away, his blood dripped on the formerly green leaves of the *deek* tree and caused them to become red, as they now are. (Wheatcroft 1976: 479). In the context of the initiation shelters set up in the forest under an *ayan* pandanus tree, the sexual message is even more explicit. Novices are made to wear a phallocrypt fashioned from the upper break of the hornbill in place of the normal gourd. A *botok* marsupial is caught and tied to the tree with belts and head-bands of shell valuables (*bonang*), and decorated with red Bird-of-Paradise feathers and red parrot feathers. Pandanus leaves are thereupon stripped from the tree to cries: 'Let them lust for you!' A large red seed, widely used by the Ok as a hunting charm, is rubbed over the novices' eyes to the spell 'may you see wealth, to pay for a wife!' Thereupon pieces of *derule* wood are brought out, one each to be tied into the pandanus wig and two each to be held in the crotch or under the thigh by the squatting novices as their pandanus wigs are being braided into their hair. These pieces of wood are referred to as 'penises', and while constructing the wigs the initiators sing the words: 'Your vaginas are there, Oh sacred *derule*, your penis tongues go into place!' Finally, the novices are painted with red ochre and juice of the red, phallic pandanus mixed in a pig's fat base, and they are brought into the village to perform the Bird-of-Paradise dance in the women's section of the village 'to arouse single women' (*ibid.*: 475ff). The other main element is the above mentioned fire-making ritual (p.5). Making fire is a male skill and prerogative, and a recognized index of a husband's duty. With the local use also made of fire as an image for passion, it does not seem far-fetched to interpret this as a similar statement in another idiom.

A roughly similar initiation seems to have been practiced also by the Telefolmin. But whereas the red colour (*towalasuk* = towal secretions, from *towal* = bright red pandanus fruit and Towalok = Afekan's brother) is seen by Tifalmin as unquestionably male, the Telefolmin secretly invert this by mixing menstrual blood in it and darkly suggesting its 'real' identity as a female substance (p.7). Thus a characteristically Ok paradox is created – the deeper significance of which there is however not sufficient available material to specify further.

In the Bimin-Kuskusmin rituals, on the other hand, we are confronted with a luxuriance both of sexual imagery and of materials. In explicit opposition to

40

the Baktaman material, 'gender contrast informs much of Bimin-Kuskusmin ethos and world view, and their instantation in everyday life' (Poole n.d.:5, and fn.15). To catch hold of the most immediately parallel features in Bimin-Kuskusmin rites to those described in the preceding paragraphs, we should search for the analogue initiations or ritual episodes and observe their local shapes and emphases. Pandanus wigs may be used as an initial indicator. Among the Bimin-Kuskusmin, pandanus wigs are employed in no less than three different major initiations. The sixth stage of initiation, where the wigs first appear, is called *saip mom*. (Poole gives no etymology for these term, but it is suggestive that the rites are organized around the sacrifice of two marsupials stuffed with taro and sweet potato respectively, and the Baktaman initiation to sacred marsupial hunting and sacrificing is named by them *sepban*; while *mom* may be cognate to Faiwol *mafom/maowm*, Barth 1975: 72). For the occasion, the novices are adorned with hornbill-beak phallocrypts[1] and 'wear a headdress elaborately fashioned from nut pandanus leaf fibers, cassowary plumes, and red cordyline leaves' (Poole n.d.: 48). The ritual itself, however, focusses on the offering of scraps of the sacrificial marsupials to the female (broken) skulls among the ancestral skulls in the temple in which the mystery takes place. A partial account is told the novices of the origins and relationships of certain marsupials, cassowary, taro and sweet potato, nut pandanus and red cordyline, while secret chants containing a fuller and more dogmatically correct account of how these life forms are related to each other through primal events of birth are also sung. Thus for example, while the chants tell how the marsupial in question is the great burrower, planter of crops, ritual ancestor of taro, and younger sibling of sweet potato, the novices are only explained that he was the first ever to wear the pandanus head-dress (*ibid.*: 49f). Towards the end of the rite, the novices also partake in sacramental commensality, eating scraps of the sacrifice.

Again in ninth degree initiation, pandanus wigs are associated with rites of sacrifice, where white substance ritually identified with the semen of a marsupial species and black substance identified as the menstrual blood of the creatress Afek are said to flow into taro. Equally vividly, feathers are taken from the novices' headdresses and inserted into the holes of female ancestral skulls, accompanied by chants disclosing that with this, Afek's vagina is closed. But in contrast to the Tifalmin rites, the sexual imagery is generalized and not directly connected with the capacities and acts of the novices themselves; and it is by the verbal cues only that the symbolism is directly linked to

---

[1] The imagery of the hornbill should be explicated. The phallus-like protuberance on its beak may be familiar to readers. Less familiar are its nesting habits: the eggs are laid in a hollow tree and when the hen starts incubating them, the male closes up the nest opening with mud till only a vertical slit remains, producing a structure rather similar to human female genitals. Through this aperture, the male regularly comes and feeds the hen by repeatedly inserting its extraordinarily shaped beak into the slit.

41

physical sexuality. In dramatic contrast to other recorded Ok rituals, however, post-menopause women are also involved as ritual leaders in these initiations.

Explicit sexual imagery, however, is most elaborate and salient in the final, tenth, initiation, including an incident where the central ridgepole of the initiation house is lowered, and identified as the penis of Yomnok, Afek's androgynous sibling and mate, sometimes represented by the flying fox. Male elders then rub white boar fat on one end of the pole, female elders rub red sow's fat on the other end. The novices carry the pole to the site of a menstrual hut, and insert it and slide it back and forth in the menstrual residues. Finally, novices are made to slide along the pole between the legs of two female elders, who hold a female ancestral skull and pour 'black blood' on them from a pig's uterus. Towards the middle of the pole, novices are supposed to masturbate and rub semen over the menstrual debris. Finally, at the other end of the pole, novices slide between the legs of male elders, who hold a male ancestral skull and cut themselves in nose, lips and tongue so 'red' blood drips on the novices as they pass. Afterwards, the novices are told an extensive myth detailing, among other things, the hermaphrodite anatomy of both Afek and Yomnok and the events whereby they gave birth to most of the ritually significant life forms, directly or through their children again, including taro, sweet potato, pandanus, cordyline, hornbill, cassowary, marsupials, spiny anteater, etc., etc. (*ibid.*: 57ff).

Whereas Poole has not himself attended or observed any of these great ritual fêtes, we must assume that they have been performed approximately as described to him. It is more difficult to be confident as regards their emotional tone and what the participants intend and experience as their overt messages and transparent innuendo. But it seems reasonable to read this Bimin-Kuskusmin material mainly as an effort to harness a range of subjective male experiences of sexuality and gender – sexual drive, repulsion, fear, nurturance, and dependence – to an epic representation of *cosmic* reproduction and life processes. This is also consistent with Weiner's independent interpretation (Weiner 1982) of a broad range of Bimin-Kuskusmin data. In comparison, Baktaman produce a far less articulated and more limited representation of growth and fertility by using gender reciprocity of wild game for cultivated crops as a metaphor in male sacrifices to ancestors; while Tifalmin address the theme of carnal attraction between the sexes, and its social regulation, with pleasurable anticipation, without explicitly connecting it with a wider fertility mystery.

It would be very simple-minded to try to interpret these respective expressions as balanced blueprints, adequate models, of or for gender relations in each different Ok group – yet this is the situation anthropologists often manoeuvre themselves into in their efforts to pursue analysis of myth or ritual. In the present case, we are dealing only with the partial views represented in a male cult. But the more general point is that in *any* representation, only some aspects of gender relations are given attention, whether as metaphors for other things or as themes in their own right. Strathern makes this point with specific reference to the sexual antagonism often discussed in connection with some New Guinea societies when she states that we 'should not *assume* for cultures that make heavy symbolic use of the antithesis between male and female that it literally divides men and women into social classes . . .' (M. Strathern 1981: 169, also cited in Poole & Herdt 1982). In the present context I would argue that we have no reason to believe that gender relations differ significantly between Baktaman, Tifalmin, and Bimin-Kuskusmin. The members of each group are posessed of the same range and qualities of experienced relations, and the same materials to employ in metaphor: the differences between their rites cannot be accounted for by isomorphic differences between their societies. I can certainly say with great conviction that gender relations, as experienced by many Baktaman, encompass a very broad emotional spectrum and a great variety of common, replicated episodes and scenarios. Some of these find expression in highly formalized cultural products, for example love-songs in a genre that boils down to blunt statements of sexual attraction and desire; others are externalized in conventional formats but depend heavily on spontaneous creativity, as for example the hour-long very moving soliloquies of women at the death of a loved person (cf. Wheatcroft 1976 for beautiful materials of this kind from Tifalmin), or recriminating harangues in crises of jealousy and infidelity; while some of the basic emotional content, e.g. of the relation between spouses, seems never to be externalized in any descriptive form, and is available to one's partner and marginally to others only in spontaneous chains of interaction which obliquely imply the love, trust, dependence etc., that constitute some of its essential elements (cf. Jorgensen's 1984: 123f. vignette of spouses playing tag for a similar view on Telefolmin marital relations).

Back to the central argument of this analysis. I would not merely contend that Baktaman, Bolovip, Tifalmin, Telefolmin and Bimin-Kuskusmin have 'chosen' different narrow aspects of their largely similar wide spectrum of gender relations and experiences to employ as idioms in their various rites. I also wish to suggest that the wide differences in gender imagery which we observe in the different cosmological sub-traditions arise from clearly identifiable processes. The starting point is provided in a basically shared wide spectrum of male experiences and emotions relating to women: sexual drive, lust, repulsion, fear, love, dependence, nurturance (cf. above, p.42ff). These provide the raw materials with which the ritual expert can work. But surely no cosmology of any one particular group can conceptualize and express all of that broad, ambivalent and terribly important relationship that obtains between man and woman in any adequate and comprehensive form. When any particular cosmologist works to reproduce and clarify the metaphors of his rituals, however, *particular features* of gender and gender roles may be seized upon as apposite, pregnant metaphors for aspects of various other relations, qualities or processes in the world: for example, the union of man and woman, represented by the union of their sexual fluids, can provide imagery for the cosmic union of forces that produces taro fertility. Certain elements of sex and gender thus become 'symbolic' in the context of the cult of fertility, ancestors and life force.

Yet it is near unthinkable that such gender-derived idioms, no matter how compelling a cosmic vision they produce, should be 'cleansed' permanently in the consciousness of ritual expert and novices of the echoes of their many other associations and connotations. The union of the sexes may be a powerful metaphor for the growth of taro, but it will inevitably also evoke other associations and meta-messages in the minds of men and boys. Thus unintended double and multiple entendre must flourish and be particularly potent in incrementally transforming both message and form of expression through the course of repeated oscillations between collective ritual performances and secret private thoughts.

A concept of 'private symbols' (cf. Obeyesekere 1981: 14ff) captures only some aspects of these events, and mystifies them unduly. The associations which such gender-derived idioms evoke in boys and men may be private, but they will surely be relatively stereotyped and easily shared; it requires only mild suggestion to indicate that I-am-also-thinking-of-what-you-are-thinking-of. The meta-levels of reference remain closely accessible, and can easily be made public and shared.

This argument is further strengthened when we remember the inevitable character of dialogue which the organization of Ok secret cult produces: the initiator acts and leads a receptive group of awed, attentive novices, and he is sensitive to their moods and reactions. At the same time, they are safely encapsulated in the context of secret rites: unsayable things may be said here.

My construction is one that would ascribe exceptional volatility to the particular meta-level of symbolism that obtains at any one time in a sub-tradition – particularly with respect to sexuality, but in principle likewise with respect to all other broadly familiar idioms. I envisage a situation where the pendulum can swing equally either way or many ways: sexual imagery may be used richly and increasingly abstractly; or the abstract metaphoric statements of cosmological rites may be read increasingly sexually to arouse erotic fantasies or express male ambivalencies of attraction and repulsion. Though individually nurtured, various interests are perennially present and ubiquitously shared; there is nothing inherently private and uncommunicable about the one and collective and intersubjective about the other. But the mere fact of the existence of a shared substratum (of lewd fantasies; or the wide occurrence of individual memories of how sexuality gave a sense of being transported in a cosmic experience; or a ubiquitous repressed resentment or fear of women) is

44

not enough. It is the particular organization of the cult that facilitates the objectification of such potentially collective ideas. The ritual expert is faced with the task to make the mystery immanent, to spellbind himself and his novices with the experience. This pressure on him gives him both the need and the freedom to articulate ideas only diffusely present in his consciousness. Through his own groping search for the essence of the mystery, he can come to objectify new modulations of the basically multivalent symbols, in a context where his statements have the full imprimatur of authority to a public of novices. Thus, by shifting meta-levels of attention and reference, particular rites within a sub-tradition can be quickly and radically transformed in imagery and key messages.

7

The stepwise articulation of a vision

The third kind of sequence of change which I claim is induced through oscillations of subjectification and objectification is perhaps most readily credible to an academic audience: that whereby the bearers of a sub-tradition pursue and develop a logical train of thought to further and new implications. Without any awareness of innovatively changing a received tradition, but merely by trying to communicate it more truly and deeply, such elaboration is profoundly stimulated by an organization where the ritual leader is required to 'show' the secrets of the cult to regularly recurring sets of new novices every ten years or so.

In trying to align and present the material to illustrate this process of generalization and abstraction, however, I am in danger of performing the abstraction myself, rather than revealing and pointing to its empirical occurrence in the tradition of knowledge I am describing. Likewise, the differences between the accounts from Tifalmin, Telefolmin, Bimin-Kuskusmin etc., may reflect differences in how far their ethnographers have gone in abstraction, and the emphases they have given, rather than empirical differences between the sub-traditions. Firth has perceptively warned us against adding our 'personal dimension to the interpretation of an alien religious ideology, to raise the generalizations to a higher power than the empirical content of material warrants' (Firth 1959: 139). To my knowledge, we have no methodology – other than perpetual vigilance and self-criticism – to help us avoid this, while much structuralist methodology entices and seduces us to the opposite. For note the purposes of the present exercise: it is intended as an exploration of the anthropology of knowledge, not the analysis of deep structure. I am concerned with the vision and knowledge that have been codified in (each of) these sub-traditions of knowledge and not the structure of the code *per se*. But is it not true, particularly of ritual, that the medium is the message? Not quite. For example, we must recognize that to show that speakers of a language use their verbs in a certain pattern of conjugations is not to show that they have concepts of 'verb' and a knowledge of 'conjugations'. When speakers of a language develop such grammatical concepts, it *changes* their tradition of knowledge, although it does not change their language. But we

46

are not truly able to answer, or even make sense of, the question whether such a population 'really' must already have known of verbs and tenses by virtue of the regularities in how they used certain words. On the other hand, surely no one can deny that much of the intellectual work performed by the whole European tradition of philosophy from Aristotle until today has been to explicate the implications of a few Indo-European languages – and yet some of their conclusions have been experienced as shattering for traditional world views?

I think this issue is at the bottom of Brunton's unease, referred to in my introductory discussion (cf. p.6), that many anthropologists impose a misconstrued order on Melanesian religion: there is a broad gray zone in anthropological accounts where we neither know what is being claimed nor what is being shown. To learn parts of an alien culture, and to provide a convenient description of it, we must sort, compress and generalize; each of these operations requires that a certain degree of abstraction is performed by us as anthropologists. To what extent are then the patterns we display reflexive of that other cultural tradition? If we are interested at all in other cultures as traditions of knowledge, these are essential questions.

But the answer is not found by asking people while doing our fieldwork in our stuttering accents, and being sceptical until they convince us verbally. I turn to a theoretically motivated ethnographer rather than a first-principles theoretican to find my concerns expressed:

Ordinarily, aboriginal religion is not represented as concerned with metaphysical problems. I am not able to share such an opinion, and think that the impression of a rather mindless participation in rites created by some works reflects the outlook of the analyst rather than that of the aborigines. A prolonged exposure to the rites comes to suggest both a depth and a dignity of outlook which may lack formulation but not reality. The implicitness – by which I mean wordlessness – of the conceptions does not detract from the kind of reality they have (Stanner 1960: 264).

The rituals which we treat here contain and articulate precisely such wordless conceptions. Even where they are associated with words – spells, myths, or verbal explanations – we can have no assurance that these words capture adequately the depth and dignity of the conceptions. So our task still remains: to put words to them which capture their genuine character and the knowledge they impart, so they can be compared among themselves for reference, clarity, scope and degree of abstraction. This we can only do by relating them to the whole context of life of which they are part, and the parts of this life where they are used besides the ritual context. This entails a great number of both theoretical and methodological issues. The present text can only sketch some conclusions, rather than the reasoning that underlies them.

To explore the stepwise elaboration (or simplification) of interpretative schemata that may have taken place within the Ok tradition of knowledge, let us first focus on the view, or theory, of history that has been conceptualized in some Ok sub-traditions – to what extent has a position been clarified in their cosmology, and what is its form and scope?

Cosmologies in the making

I have shown elsewhere (Barth 1975: 18) how Baktaman tend to locate personally remembered events in terms of space – where they happened – rather
than time – when they happened. This no doubt reflects the absence of any
calendrical system for naming points in time. But Baktaman do have a view of
certain trends over time, and of the precariousness of collective lives and
institutions as well as individual lives. They are concerned about taro fertility,
and about population, which they believe (the latter correctly, as far as I can
judge) are declining. Most strikingly and pervasively, they are concerned
about the deterioration and loss of their own religious tradition. In 1968 when
my main fieldwork among them was done, this did not reflect the impact of culture contact, which was still minimal, or mission contact, which was nil; rather,
it arose from inherent dilemmas in the organization of secret cults. I have
discussed several aspects of the practice of secrecy elsewhere (*ibid.*, esp.
pp.217–22). What the Baktaman clearly see is that by guarding knowledge
and revealing it only slowly and late in the life of new men, the various parts of
this knowledge are constantly in danger of being withheld so long and carefully
that by the sudden death of the ritual expert secrets are unexpectedly and irre-
trievably lost. Such events were exemplified in the case of several clans, who
thereby had lost their clan sacra (which the senior man had hidden in the forest
when he felt weak and unable to face their power) and special clan cult secrets.
The southeastern-most Faiwolmin group, the Augobmin, had likewise lost all
collective cult knowledge above their third degree initiation through a similar
accident. The awareness is also reflected in how a profound scepticism
(generated, I believe, by other features of the cult, cf. *ibid.*: 101–2) is frequently
formulated in the phrase: 'This was all our fathers told us before they
died'.

In a review of my Baktaman monograph, Gilsenan (1977: 13) perceptively
referred to this in terms of a concept of entropy. The Baktaman have no such
concept – they have not connected their fear of loss of secrets with other features of decline under one concept. They have not extrapolated the process
back to a point of origin, though they have myths of the beginning of things, or
forward to a logical conclusion in the end of things. Yet Gilsenan's word
'entropy' can serve as an apt way to abstract and compress so as to provide a
second-order concept of what seems involved.

Among the Telefolmin, on the other hand, there is evidence that they have
performed the intellectual work of pursuing such a logical development, and
have arrived at a conceptualization which one might label 'entropy' –
Jorgensen (n.d.: 4) does precisely that, and refers to the Telefol term *biniman*,
'to become nothing'. The different aspects of deterioriation noted by the
Baktaman, and several more, are all subsumed under this term by the
Telefolmin. Telefol spatial orientation is more centred than that of the
Faiwolmin, and a concern over encroachment of periphery on the central
village is also conceptualized in this way. The process of entropy is both pro-

48

jected backward into a time when 'Telefolmin were more numerous than they are now; men were taller; taro was larger, pigs fatter; gardens grew more quickly' (*ibid.*: 5) and forward to the ultimate end of Telefolmin society. This end is variously predicted at a time when a woman gives birth to a boy already wearing the *Mafuum* pandanus wig; or when the land of the dead is filled up with people; or when the central temple at Telefolip has been rebuilt twenty-seven times (the rebuilding of the temple is the recurrent, culminating event of initiations; and the Ok numerical systems are systems of body counting starting with the left little finger and moving across the nose to the opposite little finger at twenty-seven).[1] The secret cult of ancestors is seen as an effort, ultimately futile, to hold this increasing entropy at bay: retrieval of bones and sanctifying them as the foundation of central village strength, becomes a powerful and multivalent image of combating the dissipation and rescuing something from time.

Thus, while Baktaman at best consolidate their vision in terms of a sea change – from a better past when the ancestors were alive and taro and welfare were better, to a present time (since c. 1950) when steel axes have replaced stone axes (both obtained externally through ceremonial trade) and the blessing of ancestors has failed – Telefolmin have developed a clearer and more embracing and abstract concept from the same set of concerns and experiences.

The Bimin-Kuskusmin, on their part, have created a different and cyclical vision. Baktaman envision the beginning of human life from a kind of covenant with the original ancester Awarek – the tree-foraging, ground-burrowing 'white' marsupial who bestowed taro and instituted clan organization. Bimin-Kuskusmin myths, on the other hand, relate a history of at least three such covenants in connection with the stepwise institution of social life ordered in the fashion of present society with respect to descent and segmentation, exogamy, and territoriality (Poole 1976: 321–31, 498–507). Thus the moiety organization was introduced as a solution to the deteriorating condition of warfare and anarchy caused by tribal exogamy. A second progressive 'fall from grace' led finally to the institution of territorial rights and secret cult focussing on clan ancestors rather than pan-tribal cult. Then again, as segmentation of patriclans increased and cross-cousin marriages allowed affinal loyalties to increase, the ancestral spirits returned to institute broader bilateral rules of exogamy. While a contrast is drawn between a past when food was more plentiful, rituals more successful, people larger, etc., compared to life as it is today, the trend of deterioration is not projected to its ultimate conclusion; instead a new cycle is initiated. In harmony with this, Bimin-Kuskusmin have also

---

[1] Puzzlingly, Poole reports Bimin-Kuskusmin numbers to start with the left *thumb* but end up with the right little finger. Of the terms he cites for the fingers, only two are clearly cognate with the Faiwol terms I know, and their numerical values of course do not fit Faiwol. Number terms and equivalences do not become cognate till the number eight = elbow. (Cf. Poole 1976: 302–3).

produced an ideal conception of a circulating system of four age grades, onto which they try to fit the generations. A pervasively cyclical view of history thus resolves these existential experiences differently for the Bimin-Kuskusmin, in a conceptual development that seems uniquely their own.

We can thus recognize that the three forms exemplified here are three possible constructions over the same base of existential problems, though exhibiting different scope and degree of abstraction. However, widely based as these conceptions are in a number of collective representations, one would expect particular individuals and particular occasions (no matter how authoritative and conventionalized) to move the conceptions along one or another logical line of development by small and unnoticed steps, in the direction of more elaboration or less.

Another kind of development of a logical train of thought is that of linking an increasing number of facts or interpretations to one particular idea or schema. Thereby, the idea or schema gains in generality and validity, and progressively emerges as a more central theory in the cosmology. For example, we touched briefly above on the hot/cold dichotomy (p.33) – to what extent have local sub-traditions of Ok cosmology attempted to create a synthesis by means of this pair? I have previously speculated on the extent to which a concept of 'heat' which collapses intensity, sacredness, and fertility underlies Baktaman thought (Barth 1975: 238 fn.), but the exercise was not very conclusive. Nor do more recent materials from other Faiwol areas bring us any further. It is striking that work on the concept of illness (Jones 1980) among Faiwol has not added to our materials on hot/cold classifications. Among the Bimin-Kuskusmin, it would seem that hot is more saliently counterposed to cold; but the material so far has not clarified the extent to which a broader cosmological synthesis has been developed on this basis.

Elsewhere in New Guinea, materials are accumulating that link hot and cold with growth and decay in an elaborate vision of life process as a recycling between the two. The theme among Ok people which is typologically, if not genetically, similar, finds its key metaphors not in hot and cold but in the antithesis of nurturing and killing. I shall review briefly the lineaments of this cosmological synthesis in some of the sub-traditions.

There is a widely distributed injunction among Ok people that planting must stop in a taro garden from the moment that harvesting commences. In taro cultivation, the tops of the harvested taro must be replanted fairly shortly after they are cut. Since food crops cannot successfully be stored for long and taro is the staple food, this means that taro cultivation must be programmed so both harvesting and planting take place almost continuously. When a new garden is established, planting generally starts in one end and proceeds forward, through the months, as new stalks become available and must be planted. But once the first planted stalks have come to maturity, and are harvested, planting must

50

–

come to an end in that garden: a new garden must by then have been cleared and the activities of lifegiving and regeneration be transferred to it, and not be exposed to its antithesis of cutting and harvesting.

Likewise, there is an injunction for men – who are the persons authorized to perform the slaughter of pigs – that they cannot eat any pig they have themselves tended: all its meat must be given to others, who in turn will reciprocate when a pig they have tended is slaughtered. Women and boys may or may not observe this injunction: it is the antithesis of nurturing and killing, not the ambivalences of attachment and sentiment, which is basic. The Ok draw a specific analogy between this 'exophagy' and rules of incest and exogamy.

The reciprocities of such exchanges do not seem to engage Ok cosmological imagination particularly; it is when the inimical opposites become linked in a process of recycling that the vision becomes moving. Jorgensen reports briefly on some of the imagery developed by the Telefolmin over this theme (Jorgensen 1982 – the following passage is a somewhat compacted paraphrase of his pp.11–12). Red/white colour symbolism provides a convenient and revealing framework. The ancestor cult is internally divided into two divisions: *iman miit*, 'Taro Kind', associated with the nurturing activities of gardening and pig-raising and the colour white, and *un miit*, 'Arrow Kind', associated warfare and hunting, and the colour red. Powerful transformative processes are represented in myth and ritual as transformations between red and white. Thus (1) blood and taro must normally be kept strictly segregated – but in the final phase of the 'taro rite' initiation, a pig is slaughtered in the garden and its blood made to flow into the ground to cause the 'birth' of taro before harvest. (2) Traditional Telefolmin mortuary practice was to place the corpse on an exposure platform in one of the deceased's gardens. Thus flesh and blood will rot and fall to the earth of the taro fields and be transformed and retrieved as white taro; ultimately the transformed, white bones may also be retrieved and placed in the temple. (3) Cowries and other shell valuables used as bridewealth and mortuary payments derive mythologically from maggots in the rotting flesh of a corpse. (4) A sacred weed with a white milky sap is known as the 'Taro Vine' and used to further the growth of the taro. A secret myth reveals that the vine was originally a man's penis, which his sister cut off as an analogy to severing the umbilical cord; the original heavy flow of blood is now represented by the white sap. Finally, as noted above, according to Telefolmin women it is the mother's menstrual blood that produces the child's immortal and potentially white and sacred bones. The most sacred ancestral temple in Telefolip is dedicated to the mother-creatress Afek; the red body paint with which men celebrate their virility is really her menstrual blood, etc., etc.

The nearby Tifalmin present other convolutions. Among them, the creator-mother figure creates most life forms not by giving birth, but by killing various of her relatives. In contrast to Telefolmin and Bimin-Kuskusmin there is no suggestion that any of the ancestral bones in the temple are female, they are all

51

male. When the central temple is known as 'Amowk', House of Mother, it is because these male ancestors look after us like a mother. There is thus a reversal of primal and sacred *roles*, not substances. Corpses must *not* be placed in gardens but should, as among most Ok peoples, be exposed in tree platforms far away in the bush. There, white maggots will grow in the rotting blood and meat, fall to the ground, and become a multiplicity of marsupials (Wheatcroft 1976).

What, then, of the Faiwol materials? Whereas the north-western groups, led by Imigabip, have participated eagerly in a cult form closely similar to that of Telefolmin, organized in an Amowk (House of Mother) temple containing (as noted, p.4) female ancestral bones, a similar synthesis based on these themes does not seem to be represented further east. Bolovip distinguish between *wúname* (arrow) and *imename* (taro) ancestors in their main temple, determined by the clan identity of the respective ancestors; they are kept apart to the left and the right along the sacred wall of the temple and are decorated with red and white colour respectively; but transformations and inversions of the colours are less in evidence. Colour symbolism, among them as among the Baktaman, focusses on a multivocal consistency, basically of red = descent, virility, war and white = taro, wealth (shell valuables), prosperity. Both are aspects of ancestral blessing; indeed, among the Baktaman there is no antithesis between them and the central ancestral skull in the Yolam temple may be painted, at different occasions, with a red line, a white line, or both, on his forehead.

Quite clearly, a synthesis has been developed in the west and north which the southeastern people lack. Indeed, certain features of Ok cult organization to which I have so far not given explicit attention can help us sort out this picture. There are, in most Mountain Ok villages and regions, not just one type of Haus Tamberan/Spirit House (in the widely shared idiom of Neo-Melanesian), but several distinctive sacred houses, organizing different forms of male cult. At the time of my fieldwork among the Baktaman the 54 partly or fully initiated Baktaman men had no less than three different kinds of sacred houses: the *Kaweram* (Hornbill House), men's houses with minor sacra and trophies of the hunt; the *Katiam* (Taro House), also a house of residence but only for senior men, with clan sacra; and the *Yolam* (Ancestor House) with skulls and longbones employed in the communal cult. Until recently, they had also had an *Amowkam* (House of Mother), which however was destroyed by enemy action around 1958. Each of these sacred houses served different ritual functions and articulated somewhat different visions and syntheses of cosmological ideas – but for the same congregation. The graded initiations served as a stepwise induction to them all, though each particular step of initiation tended to focus on one or another of the temples.

A similar nomenclature of cult houses is fairly widely distributed among Mountain Ok communities, though equivalences in terms of equipment and practices are less readily established, and more illusory, the greater the distance covered. Bimin-Kuskusmin, as well as some other groups, further-more employ temporary shelters of great ritual importance in some of their initiations.

It would seem that the particular synthesis I have discussed above has been associated with *one* of these cult house forms, viz.: the Amowk. This indicates an alternative way in which innovation and diffusion may take place: a new kind of temple may arise, in which themes and syntheses which are incompat-ible with established rites and temples may be developed and pursued. Indeed, distributional and other evidence suggest that the Amowk among the Faiwolmin was precisely such a recent introduction (see Barth 1971) – one might almost see it as a new sect movement spreading into a population, except that its adoption does not require the abandonment of other cult houses and practices, only the addition of the new one. But it is striking that while this Amowk articulation of cosmological ideas in various modulations is central to Telefolmin, Tifalmin, Wopkaimin and the Faiwolmin of Imigabip, it does not seem to have had any lasting attraction to the rest of the Faiwolmin. It never penetrated further east than the Baktaman, where it was added at the end of the initiation sequence; and no attempt was made to rebuilt the Amowk culthouse after 1958.[2] Their Seltaman neighbours to the west had the closest available Amowk temple – but it had been in disuse for a number of years, after its ritual expert died and no one felt competent or motivated to reopen the cult. The next Amowk temple toward the west was in Bolovip, where its associated initiation was incorporated in the middle of the sequence, as fourth or fifth step. But the 'original' Amowk of Bolovip was destroyed by their western neighbours, the Golgobip, in war. They then made a new one, with the bones of their present ritual leader's own mother. Then some time around 1955–60 it burned down, by accident; and since then nobody has tried to resurrect it. I venture the sug-gestion that these externally caused destructions do not provide the full explanation for the disappearance of this recently introduced institution from such a considerable area. During the same period, other kinds of cult houses have been reactivated, rebuilt after fires, and even established in new localities. Rather, I would suggest that the basic themes and idioms of the Amowk-associated cult were too much at odds with local concepts and sensibilities to be successfully integrated in their cult life. The ideas of strictly patrilineal descent and identity, and a strong male cult of garden fertility as a blessing from male ancestors, had, in these areas, achieved a synthesis which

---

[2] At the time of my fieldwork in 1968, an initiation set was impatiently waiting for an opportunity to be initiated into this highest, seventh degree, thereby gaining authorization to eat wild boar and play drums. Revisiting Baktaman in 1982, I found that a rather pro forma initiation had finally been arranged for them, in a temporary building in the now abandoned settlement of Kasanmin, belonging to the dialect group to the north.

53

was too threatened and troubled by the evocative imagery based on the fusions and inversions of male and female substances.

We thus seem to have uncovered a slightly different mechanism composed of diffusion, development and differentiation in this example. While the articulation of secret, sacred syntheses of cosmological lore is still dependent on the initiative and elocutionary ability of particular ritual leaders, these leaders are not limited to the transmission and incremental modification of pre-established rites: they are also provided a set of options in the institutions of known neighbouring groups, whose particular cult house types and practices they can adopt in addition, not replacement, to their own. In the typically pragmatic fashion of the Mountain Ok, there is no dogmatic objection to trying such new cult varieties and seeing their efficacy on local gardens, pigs and people, so long as they do not do too gross violence to taboos and rules which are regarded as constitutive to the practice of already established rites. Even this caveat is most elastic, because of the recognized role of secret paradox and inversion. It allowed, for example, the all-male secret cult groups of the Faiwolmin to try out the sanctification of women's bones as ancestral relics, and menstrual pollutants as sources of power, in new attempts to control vegetative fertility. But within each sub-tradition, some kind of longer-term criteria of consistency do seem to operate, whereby cult is harnessed to a search and a struggle to build a cosmological vision of some measure of coherence and force. I see a very challenging program in trying to ascertain more explicitly what the canons of coherence and persuasiveness are in such a tradition of knowledge.

8

Experience and concept formation

The thesis I am pursuing is not intended to oppose a Durkheimian perspective with the simplistic observation that cultural form and practice are ultimately the work of individuals. Quite clearly, Mountain Ok cosmology is produced and reproduced by collective social processes. But an adequate model of any social process requires an account of individual activity as well as group activity. Moreover, such a model should identify causal links, and not mere correlations or isomorphies, between forms of ritual and forms of society. In preceding chapters I have shown that particular features of the social organization of the Ok cosmological tradition of knowledge are such as to stimulate and canalize individual creativity and performance in ways which profoundly affect the collective rites and symbols of this tradition. Thus, I claim to have uncovered processes that generate a proliferation and diversity of cosmological schemes. I shall now try to trace some other kinds of causal links between social organization and cult forms. Some features of these cult forms may be regarded as the fruits of particular constellations of organizational features; in other cases the organizational features may best be understood as an *effect* of certain religious ideas and ritual practices. I shall sketch these connections first with respect to the organization of clans in the Faiwol area, where religious ideas and practices seem to be formative of important features of social organization. Next, I shall try to show that the spectacular elaboration of myth as a modality of expression among Telefolmin and Bimin-Kuskusmin, and its absence among Faiwolmin, are more readily understood as the consequence, rather than the cause, of associated organizational features.

First, to descent organization and descent groups. We have already noted the presence of bilateral kindred as the basic units of organization among the western and northern Mountain Ok (though, apparently, not further west in the Star Mountains, cf. Pouwer, 1964), in contrast to the patrilineal clans found to the south and east. The thesis I shall seek to demonstrate is that this structure of patrilineal descent emerges as a consequence of the form of ancestor cult practiced in the *Katiam* type cult house, and is a derivative accomplishment, not a primary social fact that can be used as a premise for social and cultural analysis.

55

Cosmologies in the making

A number of observations made during fieldwork suggested that there was something problematic and indecisive about Baktaman clan organization. It is not that the presence of features used as anthropological criteria for clanship is in doubt. Every person among the Baktaman is provided with an unalterable identity as a member of a named descent group by virtue of his or her father's membership in this group. Clans are dispersed, and have political implications only to the extent that a person may not kill a clansman or see his blood be shed – he must turn his face away when this happens. But all sexual relations, and therefore also marriage, are banned between members of such a group, no matter how distantly related or unrelated they may be. As noted, the very origins of human life and taro cultivation are traced to an explicit instruction to this effect by the original ancestor. But this singleminded anthropological abstraction of features which define 'a patrilineal clan organization' from their context in Baktaman life does violence, at the very outset, to the nature and significance of 'clan' identity: the anthropologist's criteria for 'clan' and 'patrilineal descent' are not incisive emic concepts among the Faiwolmin.

To begin with, there is no unambiguous term for 'clan' in Faiwol. Various images may be used: *nangar* (shoulder, also the lower ridges, i.e. base, of a mountain) or *mit* (trunk-and-main-roots of a tree) are most common. But it always proved difficult verbally to bring up clanship as a topic of conversation: much misunderstanding would ensue. What is more, children and many women were genuinely unsure of the name of their own clan. Within the area of the c. 3000 speakers of Faiwol, there is also very significant variation in the forms and salience of clanship. Men from the closest neighbouring communities east of the Baktaman were particularly reluctant to reveal their clan identity to me, and apparently to other outsiders, and were extremely secretive about clan cult; while the communities in the far south-east seem to lack such groups (cf. Barth 1971: 178). Communities further west, on the other hand, fail to enforce clan exogamy properly, as in Bolovip, or do not require exogamy, as in Imigabip. The material thus provokes the question which should, on purely theoretical grounds, have been fundamental to any discussion of descent in New Guinea or elsewhere, but which is rarely explicated: what are the sets of experiences, and the concept formations, that make people *embrace* clan identity and enforce rules with reference to such membership?

In other words, I am not merely raising the question of what the idioms are, what the ideology is, and how actual groups are composed, as in the debate on 'African models' in the New Guinea Highlands (esp. Barnes 1962, de Lepervanche 1967–8, Strathern 1972); I am asking what makes the identity personally compelling. One can immediately sense the difference between many patrilineally organized peoples in the Middle East, Africa, or the Roman gens, from the situation among the Faiwolmin. Among the former, the individual members' consciousness can have no chance of escaping the vast, self-confirming structure of law, politics and property, supported by a pattern of domestic organization and daily activity, whereby it is self-evident that 'I am' a member by ascription of a certain descent group (cf. Barth 1973). Among the Faiwolmin on the contrary, with hamlet-based political and legal sodalities, no experience of domestic coresidence between father and children, very little lineal transmission of rights, and poorly developed notions of time, genealogy and history, nothing like this is self-evident. The anthropologist cannot merely return to Rivers (1924: 86–8) and restate the condition that recruitment should occur automatically, by virtue of birth alone. Nowhere does it occur automatically; but in some societies every legitimate birth occurs in a context where these vast structures are invariably *entailed*. Among the Baktaman, on the other hand, the social reality of such a birth position is only laboriously, obliquely and unevenly induced.

The work whereby it is achieved, and the concepts whereby it is objectified, are found in the Katiam temple. Let us look at some of the specifics in the Baktaman case (cf. Barth 1975, esp. 109–12). In 1968 the Baktaman had one major, and one smaller Katiam. The most sacred parts of a Katiam are the fire(s); the inner wall progressively covered with wild boar skulls and mandibles, and cassowary pelvises, from sacrifices; and hidden among them, the sacra *par excellence*: small, tightly woven string bags containing the relics of clan ancestors. In the larger Katiam, there were six such relic shrines, in the smaller there was one. The bones of the relics should be fingerbones, mandible, clavicle or sternum – never skull or longbones – and the deceased is not represented as an apical ancestor of the clan or local segment of the clan, only as a powerful, deceased member, though each seems to be thought of as a representation of *all* clan ancestors of his particular clan. The larger Katiam contained three shrines of Minkarin clan, and one each of Yabik, Yeni and Murukmur. The small Katiam contained one shrine of Wanfaghar clan (see p.58).

Only the eleven fully initiated men were allowed to reside in, or regularly enter, the Katiam because of the sacredness of these shrines; but a further fifteen men of the next lower initiation grade had attended several important rites there, while 28 young men had once attended a ritual there, though without having the clan relics identified. Each shrine has its special keeper or priest; only he can open the string bag and handle the bones. The keeper should be a senior member of the clan; but since the Murukmur had no fully initiated member, the senior Minkarin man was also temporary caretaker for the Murukmur shrine, while because of previous personal intrigues and rivalries, the senior Yabik man was caretaker for the third Minkarin shrine, as well as keeper of his own Yabik shrine. The remaining 128 Baktaman had no access to any aspect of clan cult and essentially no knowledge of its existence or its sacra.

Each clan has its traditional point of origin in a sink hole, usually in distant territory (further west, some or most groups – whether patrilineal or bilateral – trace their origins from Telefolip). These places of origin are not widely

Cosmologies in the making

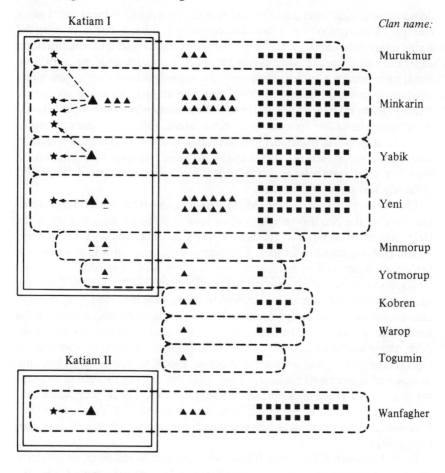

★ clan shrine
▲ clan priest
↖ guardianship to shrine
▲▲▲ fully initiated men, residents in Katiam
▲▲▲ partly initiated men, at least once participants in Katiam rites
■■■ uninitiated persons
⌐ ¬ membership of a clan

Figure 1: Degrees of participation in the Katiam clan cults among the Baktaman in 1968.

58

known, however, and there are no rituals connected with them. The cult acts which take place in connection with the Katiam are two: (a) Secret hunts are initiated by the Katiam leader and led by one of the eleven seniors, but with participation from the associated group of fifteen men of lower initiation grade. Through these hunts, sacrificial marsupials (and certain birds and snakes) are obtained which the seniors offer to clan ancestors by burning parts, while other parts are consumed in sacramental meals. (b) Burning in the sacred fire is performed individually of *all* bone remains – other than the skulls, mandibles and pelvises mentioned – from wild boar and cassowary that have been felled and consumed. A competent and active hunter may produce a considerable volume of bone materials for such cremation. These bones are usually dried for more conventional disposal and progressively fed into the fires of the Katiam. The theology that ordains these particular rites need not concern us; I am concerned only to give sufficient detail so we can form an appreciation of the kind of subjective meaning and identity the clan cult generates. For this, its overt purpose is very important: the meticulous observation of clan cult is above all believed to secure hunting luck, so a man can satisfy his wife and feed himself, her and their children; it is also supposed to secure the fertility of taro gardens of clan members and perhaps, more diffusely, of all Baktaman.

The basic conceptions associated with the Katiam are somewhat at odds with those of the central, Yolam temple. According to Baktaman ethnohistory, they once lived dispersed in clans, and it was the Yolam cult that constituted them as a nucleated village (Barth 1971: 184ff). In Bolovip, the Yolam cult gives greater recognition to clanship: in the division of ancestor skulls and clans into 'arrow' and 'taro' kinds, and the rule that you can only sacrifice to the skull of your own (father's) clan, or if there is no skull from it represented, then that of your mother's or grandmother's patriclan. No such rules are observed by the Baktaman, and their one exemplary ancestral skull combines the red and white colours of both 'arrow' and 'taro'. Among the Baktaman, at least, one might say that the articulation of clan identity is constantly being overbid by the pan-village message of the more prestigious Yolam cult. Yet for the senior men it would seem that their own feeling of commitment is greatest to the Katiam cult – perhaps because they must do its more modest rituals themselves, separately and more frequently. Moreover, its immediate relevance is to the ubiquitous issue of hunting luck – which also critically entails their masculinity and their relation to their wife – rather than the more abstract question of taro fertility.

The relics, though constant companions in the house of residence, are regarded with the greatest reverence – to such an extent that any manipulation and adjustment of the cult becomes very difficult. Thus, once the relics of the Warop clan were lost, no new shrine was established although potential relics of Warop clan members are in fact available in the collective cave necropolis of the Baktaman. Likewise, the clans of three very important senior men were without relics. Only in Bolovip do I know of a recent case of creating a clan shrine. This was done two years before my 1982 visit by the mercurial ex-headman of Bolovip, who fetched a bone supposedly of one of his own Lumkai ancestors from Telefolmin, and installed it in Selabip hamlet, where one of his six wives and a group of his junior clan mates live. It is essential to recognize the deeply ambivalent attitudes of respect, fear, dependence and exultation that surround the sacra and one's own role in approaching and worshipping them; but an essential component derives precisely from the conviction that they are *not* man-made products that can be created by one's own work.

But what *is* the fruit of one's own work, so directly that it is not to do violence to Baktaman consciousness to emphasize it, is one's own *commitment*. Clanship obtains its importance to these old men because of the clan cult. The problem is, here the old men are out of tune with the generally prevailing consciousness of the rest of the Baktaman. It is not merely that some old men know something, and have a theory, that others do not know. That can be a great strength, particularly given the kinds of premises about secrecy and sacredness to which Mountain Ok generally subscribe. The problem is, in the clan, they are dealing with an object which hardly exists apart from its secret objectification. Taro gardens, game, any kind of food have an import of great significance in a Faiwol populance, and almost automatically generate great interest and excitement – so any secret theory about such objects has a pre-established importance. Gender differences, generations, villages, etc., are there, as existential givens, and provide ready materials for metaphorization and mysteries. Even the imposed practice of a taboo or a conventional habit creates a substratum of experience which can later provide the material for metaphor and tortuous significance. But 'clan' hardly emerges as a category by virtue of *any* experience outside of the Katiam. Even the abstention represented by exogamy is obscure, where populations are small and all cousins are within the prohibited degrees. And yet, in Faiwol epistemology, it is precisely the secrecy which lends force to the conception.

Thus, a situation is created where the vision and commitment of a handful of senior men must be sufficiently strong to make it necessary for them to impose this ephemeral group identity on a vastly larger, ritually passive population which has no experience that calls for its conceptualization.

Why do the old men chose to impose *exogamy* as the public mark of this identity? The rightness of this marker, from their point of view, must spring from two sources. (a) It provides a 'self-evident' image for unity and closeness (there is no significant development of concepts of alliance that would provide ambiguity to this imagery). (b) More specifically, clan cult is the secret, mystical source of hunting luck, coterminous with male potency. There is an uneasy, haunting male awareness that to keep a wife it is necessary to 'satisfy' her, and the gender role is one that collapses meat provision, and giving sexual satisfaction, as the essentials of potency. Thus turning such clan powers inward onto women of the clan would be the essence of incest.

I therefore maintain my argument that it is the practice of a particular form of cult of ancestors that generates in senior men a conception of clan identity that necessitates exogamous clans. This causal chain is precarious, in real life. Slightly different ideas of the duties connected with these ancestors could easily have the result that less commitment is generated in these senior men, with which to draw an unenlightened population into the observation of clan identity. Other differences in the ideas can easily lead to changed conceptions of the benefits that are supposed to flow from ancestor cult. Reducing the salience of hunting luck reduces the relevance of exogamy as a feature of clan identity, and thereby leads to agamous patriclans, as among some Mountain Ok groups, or to the endogamous kindred formations found among other Mountain Ok.

Besides springing from the perspective adopted in the preceeding chapters, this conception owes something to Weiner's inspiring analysis of Poole's Bimin-Kuskusmin materials (Weiner 1982). I had previously described the Baktaman situation too exclusively from the 'informed' position of seniors. I also found her formulation most seminal when she observes: 'Ancestral attachments are not automatically formed at a person's birth. They must be produced through the work of men's initiation rituals and through the work of birth as culturally perceived' (*ibid.*: 58). In the rather different context of Bimin-Kuskusmin involvement of (post-menopausal) clan *sisters* as participant ritual leaders in male initiation and cults, Weiner builds her analysis on an inclusive concept of 'reproduction' which subsumes, as I understand it, not only giving birth and recreating social relations, but also the recreation of any form of intersubjective values and knowledge, both the objects which serve as their concrete symbols and the attitudes which these concrete symbols validate (*ibid.*: 64). The difficulty that arises from this conception is that it collapses material and symbolic work in a metaphor that easily disguises the very different constraints under which such different work must be done. I have tried in the above discussion to provide enough ethnographic detail to illustrate just how difficult it can be to bring off symbolic work. It is not enough to put in the hours and days of fussing over some bones and presto! the group has the relics it needs for its objectification. Not only must audiences and effects be created in concrete contexts; particular events constantly trip up the project, because life does not bow to the schemata of symbols to the same extent that it does to physical work. So the Baktaman must always be unsure of the force of their images, and they are easily left adrift, robbed of their capacity to act – e.g. because a particular bone has been lost by a befuddled old man. The capacity to reach closure, to assert a conception which is publicly compelling, can sometimes be far more precarious than other times; and there are causal connections, outside of the coded symbols, that must be identified by us as anthropologists and used to explain such differences. But in some contexts, these may enhance rather than restrict the implications of symbolic schemata. Therefore we cannot affirm 'the limitations of bones to regenerate more than ancestors' (*ibid.*: 64): there can be circumstances, as I hope I have shown, when organizations of exogamous clans emanate from the work done on such bones.

The other causal connection announced in the opening of this chapter leads in the opposite direction *from* social organization *to* the mode of expression in cult. It is a simpler idea, but also far more tentative. The problem is posed by the variation in the communicative modalities in which Mountain Ok cosmology is cast in the different sub-traditions. Whereas all show a prolific elaboration of ritual acts and collective ritual performances, the extend of use of myth and other forms of verbal expression in connection with cult is highly variable. On the one hand, I have emphasized the remarkable poverty of myths, and even of spells and verbal explanations in accompaniment to initiation and instruction, among the Baktaman. A similar poverty seems to prevail in most Faiwol areas. This does not reflect any general failure of verbal articulateness: both in informal intercourse and in more formalized situations of recounting, explaining, haranguing or lamenting, persons appear quite articulate. But their notions of secrecy, and also respect and reserve, surrounding the sacred seem to inhibit nearly all verbalization of sacred tradition even in the context of its ritual performance and in contexts where only fully authorized and initiated persons are present as an audience. The effective constraints in the latter cases as seen by the Baktaman are two: dangerous forces are let loose by mentioning them, and the consequences are unpredictable but probably bad; secondly, invisible spirits are probably present, some of them pernicious, while ancestral spirits who are most certainly present might be angry that sacred things connected with them were discussed idly.

Among the Telefolmin and Tifalmin, on the other hand, things are somewhat different. The ideas of sacredness and secrecy continue to be closely joined. Yet there seems to be a large corpus of lore – myths and stories of various kinds. Though these are secret, there naturally must be occasions when they are told, or they would not exist. The anthropologist's first problem then is to gain access to them – optimally by being integrated into the exclusive circles of authorized persons who should share the secrets. Presumably, they serve both as exegesis for certain rites, and as a modality of expression, to appropriate audiences, in their own right.

The materials from Bimin-Kuskusmin are even more striking. Poole documents that truly epic myth cycles are known among them. These are recited at certain set points in the rituals of initiation; and they also seem allowed to be retold to competent audiences at other occasions, so long as they are kept secret from the unauthorized. I also understand Poole's claim to be that the kinds of conversational explanation and exegesis he elicited, especially from his chief informant Firemsok, were largely within a tradition of verbal instruction practiced among the Bimin-Kuskusmin themselves, and not entirely an innovation provoked by Poole. In place of the pregnant silences of Faiwolmin rites, with low whispers of only the most essential instructions to novices or congregations, and the absence of more than a small body of essential myths, we thus find among some other Mountain Ok groups a flourishing tradition of perhaps several distinct genres of sacred verbal discourse. Why?

The answer, I would suggest, is found in the differences in the social organization of the various sacred sub-traditions. All of them are based on secrecy; axiomatically, one would expect strong constraints on verbal communication about sacred matters to be in operation. But the Faiwolmin social organization of the sacred tradition is such that it allows these constraints to be elevated to an almost universally practicable dogma. Initiations are performed by one person or a very small college of senior persons on homogeneous cohorts of novices. Numbers are small, personal supervision can be continuous. To minimize the dangers of disclosure, it is both meaningful and feasible to reduce verbal communication drastically, both for purposes of coordination and instruction.

Among the Telefolmin, Tifalmin and Wopkaimin, on the other hand, initiations and congregations are organized differently. The sequence in which higher initiations are attended is variable, and a person's participation depends on his own initiative. Thus the audiences to higher initiations are far from homogeneous, and one can envisage a need for more contextual, verbal information. More significantly, temples are organized in a hierarchy: local temples for lower initiations and everyday rituals, higher temples serving a larger area for higher initiations and the great festivals. Including the central Amdolol in Telefolip, there are at least three such hierarchical levels, entailing the presence in some temples at some times of very large numbers of very heterogeneous participants ranging from high priests through delegations of leaders of lower temples to inexperienced novices.

Bimin-Kuskusmin organization is even more elaborate. All initiations for a total population of c. 1000 persons are coordinated from the very first step. Three levels of population – native, associated and vanquished clans – are distinguished. All clans are grouped in two moieties, with differentiated and alternating ritual tasks. Among the natal clans, one clan in each moiety is regarded as ritually pre-eminent and has special functions. Within each cohort of novices, a select portion of around one third receives special instruction at each level, so as to learn the rites better and become an elite group among whom future male ritual leaders will be selected. Finally, some women – both virgins and post-menopause – from each clan are given a variety of ritually essential functions. We lack any account of how these women perceive their parts, and the whole in which they participate: it retains, after all, its basic character of a secret male fertility mystery, counterposed to the natural fertility of women and only slowly revealed to men through ten steps of elaborate initiations. But we can certainly see the necessity in this elaborate organization of explications, instructions, and special renderings of sacred information suitable for a variety of different audiences and addressed to the problem of providing them, from their particular premises, each with an integrated and compelling vision. It would seem simply not practicable to base such communications on an entirely or predominantly non-verbal code. Verbalization is so vastly more flexible, economical of time, space and equipment, and (where necessary) unambiguous, it would seem essential in orchestrating and motivating such composite performances to rely heavily on it.

Telefolmin organization would thus seem to invite a certain amount of collegiate discussion and elite elaboration of myth and other verbal sacred performance within the sequestered group of temporarily united ritual experts in the higher temples. Bimin-Kuskusmin organization seems positively to require such verbal modalities, besides the non-verbal ritual acts. Faiwol organization, on the other hand, has a character that allows an extreme concentration on non-verbal communicative forms in their sacred performances. Whichever direction one imagines development to have proceeded, it would seem that it is the organizational features that set the parameters, and the elaborations of different communicative modalities that follow.

9

The insights pursued by Ok thinkers

To press my analysis one step further, I need to generalize and abstract from the materials we have uncovered. I shall focus on two tasks: (1) to define the subject-matter of Ok cosmological constructs – what are the phenomena in the cosmos which are given systematic attention? and (2) to characterize the kinds of understanding and insight that are produced in this tradition of knowledge. Only when we are able to characterize these substantive features do we arrive in a position where we can ask further questions of 'why?': we need a clear formulation of just what it is that we wish to explain.

Questions which have preoccupied Mountain Ok cosmologists in the present century seem to have been articulated in two distinct and partly opposed positions. On the one hand, many Ok hold that an elaborate and correct male cult of ancestors generates a sacred force of growth and fertility which overcomes and replaces carnal female fertility and provides the basis for constituting organized society. Alternatively, others hold that the source of life force lies in the synthesis of a purified male principle, regulated and granted through male cult of the ancestors, and an immanent female principle represented by female substances. The former position is characteristic of the Faiwolmin. The latter position has had its centre in Telefolmin and has had a heavy impact west- and southward on Tifalmin, Wopkaimin, and the fringe of the Faiwolmin. It also saw a brief expansion into most of the rest of Faiwolmin areas through the spread of Amowk temples, probably in the period 1910–50, before a reconsolidation of the former view caused a decline in interest and activity in the Amowk cult. In the 'rat theme' in Bolovip, which I noted above (pp.20–2), we see a weak and marginal rendering of ideas from this latter position.

Among the Bimin-Kuskusmin, features of both these major positions seem to have been synthesized; but the picture is unclear because we lack materials on the connections between religious conceptions and the everyday life of communities and significant status categories within them. Particularly enigmatic are the understandings and self-conceptions of the female initiators employed in advanced steps of the secret male cult by the Bimin-Kuskusmin. Among Faiwolmin also, women do have certain functions in connection with initiations (see Barth 1975: 53, 65, 75, 87, and *Imen-Dap* 115f.) But these are

65

marginal and concerned with limited and specific functions, where women may be called as participants while remaining entirely ignorant of the occult significance of what they are doing. An entirely different form of participation is entailed in Bimin-Kuskusmin usage, wherein women, themselves uninitiated, are involved as initiators in relation to men who are moving through the higher grades of the system. This seems fundamentally at odds with the very premises on which stepwise initiation is based and the authority of elders is reproduced (cf. La Fontaine 1977: 434 for a succinct statement of the entailments of initiations). To resolve such questions we are particularly in need of an account of how female ritual leaders obtain the considerable knowledge and lore which is needed to assume an active role in the proceedings, and how their authority to possess it is ideologically justified, and comes to be embraced by themselves.

These various views on the sources of fertility serve as charters for the rituals performed in Mountain Ok temples, rituals which might perhaps most aptly be characterized as increase ceremonies for crops and youths. But this means that they serve as 'theories' of fertility, rather than as comprehensive summaries or definitions of the objects of knowledge addressed in rituals. Nor must we indeed forget the very frequently recurring, though relatively minor, rituals connected with the Katiam as a hunting lodge, whereby all cassowary and wild pig bones (other than temple trophies) should be burned in the sacred fire to ensure perpetuation of game/hunting success, and the importance of sacrifices to the ancestors in stimulating the ancestors to 'release' game and thus provide success in all secular hunting. These concerns for the ritually correct treatment of different kinds of game is the hunting counterpart of the nurturing vs. killing dichotomy of gardening and harvesting; and it is at least outwardly reminiscent of the rituals whereby boreal hunters seek to maintain and increase the game on which they depend.

While Mountain Ok rituals seem to be engaged in a constant readdressing of the problems of fertility and of killing, the substantive content of the cosmology they teach can thus be recognized as much wider: it composes a complex lore of the life forms that surround these Ok horticulturalists in their mountain slope environment. The tradition of knowledge is concerned with essentially all vertebrate species in the biota of the region, and many of its invertebrates and plants, besides the domesticated species, especially taro, sweet potato (among the Bimin-Kuskusmin) and pandanus. It thus embraces an elaborate ethnozoology and ethnobotany, in a multi-layered structure of mystical relationships, associations and equivalences between the numerous taxa.

It is characteristic that few of these relationships could by any stretch of the term be called totemic. Admittedly, some associations are posited between particular kin groups and particular animals among the Wopkaimin, according to my own data, and rather extensively among the Bimin-Kuskusmin, according to Poole. But the vast body of lore is directed at Nature itself as its object of

66

scrutiny and explanation; and the model employed is neither one which relates categories in nature to social categories, nor does it employ social models significantly as templates for relations in nature. Rather, Mountain Ok cosmologists construct a model of complex and hidden systems of circulating substances in life forms, a kind of comprehensive physiology or *alchemy of life forces* animating the world around them. Human participation and a measure of control of these processes are only precariously achieved, by means of the secret cult of ancestors and the support obtained from them through sacrifice.

Only marginally connected with cult activities but salient in popular consciousness, an additional sector of cosmology must be included to make this description empirically complete: the Mountain Ok also populate their world with a great number of invisible or fleetingly visible spirits of various kinds. These are perhaps best thought of as an additional part of the fauna of the jungle. Ubiquitous and frequently encountered, these spirits are active and interfering agents in causing sickness and accident, but occasionally also luck and individual success (see esp. Barth 1975: 124–43).

There seem to be very great differences between the cultural regions of the world in the substantive foci to which cosmologies are directed. While society and social relations are central to many traditions, expressed in a wide variety of modes from ancestor worship to witchcraft beliefs, others give privileged attention to astrology and geomancy, or matters of morality, justice and punishment. Indeed, an orientaton which selects 'Nature' as the object of sacred knowledge is probably unusual. But it reflects very adequately the consuming interest and attention which the Mountain Ok direct towards the life forms that surround them. There is a surprising lack of interest and a poverty of ideas in contemporary anthropology concerning possible reasons for differences in cosmological orientation as between different cultures; and I do not wish to enter prematurely into a comparative discussion. More usefully, let us next shift our attention from the substantive object of cosmological knowledge and understanding among the Ok to the question of what *kind* of knowledge and understanding this tradition produces. On the basis of the materials presented so far, am I able to characterize the Mountain Ok tradition of cosmological knowledge in this respect?

I have provided illustrations of the kinds of associations, equivalences, and mystical relations which this tradition of knowledge posits. The general term I must use to characterize these constructions is 'metaphor'. Thus, in the Red Bird of Paradise the Tifalmin see a metaphor embodying the ambivalences of jealousy, attraction, and the battle of the sexes, as rendered in the myth of Afek's murder of her seductive brother – because the Bird of Paradise aptly embodies the essence of beauty and seduction in its male courting dance, and because its feathers are red as blood. In the Megapod's white eggs buried in the nest mound of refuse, the Baktaman see a metaphor for their white taro, maturing in the ground, under influence of a force of growth working like the heat of decomposition, until clean food emerges from dirty ground like birds of the sky emerging from the nest mound (Barth 1975: 235f). The imagery can be experienced as moving and beautiful; some of its force survives the translation to our idioms; and it has undeniable 'meaning'. But the dance of the Bird of Paradise tells us little about the wellsprings of masculinity, and the nesting behaviour of Megapods provides a false theory of agronomy. The connections on which Ok knowledge builds its structures seem like those of rhymes and puns – they somehow 'feel' compelling and right, but they are based on fortuitous analogies of colour, location, shape, behaviour, and function.

Yet, it is conceivable that these constructs may be embedded in a context of praxis where they obtain a better founded validity. Let me take an example. Baktaman, when they weed their taro gardens, pile the uprooted weeds (other than those species which have the capacity to take root again) around the taro plants 'because taro likes the smell of rotting vegetation'. I presume this mulching both enhances the humus content around the taro roots and inhibits weed germination and growth. What is the difference between the former and the latter formulation of the relationship? In the context of this particular praxis, the Baktaman idiom seems an adequate way to depict a certain beneficial agronomical technique. My sentence, on the other hand, attempts to relate the phenomenon to a number of more general relationships, and various sciences that treat the chemistry of matter, life processes etc. – in other words to an elaborate tradition of knowledge built on consistency, generalization, deduction, experiment and measurement. The Baktaman, in the context of their own conventions of discourse, do not perform such operations on or with their statements, and thus do not in effect lay claim to possess a universal science. It therefore makes no sense to fault them as if they had made such claims for their knowledge, nor to congratulate them as if they had a covert knowledge of chemistry, biology and agronomy. The critical question is the conceptual use which *they* make of their imagery – mainly the scope which is implicitly claimed for its validity by generalizing it and uniting it with models for other connections and relationships. There is evidence that Baktaman, within their own tradition of knowledge, make *some* generalizations beyond this context of mulching, and thus connect their interpretation into a larger system of knowledge which we may call their cosmology. Thus, in some other contexts they hold that taro can not only smell but also hear, i.e. taro are regarded as generally sentient creatures; that taro and people are similar in certain ways; that the growth of taro is influenced by ancestral spirits who can in turn be influenced by properly performed sacrifices presented to ancestral skulls; etc. Our task in studying their tradition of knowledge must be to map out these generalizations and purported connections, *together with* the constraints of praxis and convention in terms of which such knowledge is applied, so as to

68

provide an accurate picture of the conceptual use which is made of the metaphors and models.

To depict Ok cosmology with any degree of accuracy, we must thus avoid templates that radically de-contextualize Ok cosmological statements. In an anthropological tradition going back to Frazer and beyond, it might seem uncontroversial to see Ok cosmology as a system of 'beliefs' about the world. But our concept of 'belief' entails exactly those assumptions of generality of truth which we need to avoid. This is aptly illustrated in the instructive debate on 'Virgin birth' where Leach (1967) is critical precisely of these anthropological constructions of de-contextualized, universal models of the thought systems of other cultures; but by retaining a terminology focussing on beliefs he is driven to speak in terms of distinctions between beliefs that are factually true – and therefore apparently more wholeheartedly embraced by believers – vs. religious dogmas which are somehow very important but not really believed. More than a decade later, the difficulties are still not resolved, and Southwold tries the same distinction in terms of factual truth vs. symbolic truth (Southwold 1979: 635). In sympathy with what I understand these authors to intend, I urge that the issues can be better approached with more suitable concepts.

For this purpose, Weber's definition of culture (of which Obeyesekere makes felicitous use, cf. Obeyesekere 1981: 106ff) provides a helpful perspective: 'Culture is a finite segment of the meaningless infinity of the world process, a segment on which *human beings* confer meaning and significance' (Weber 1949: 81). Or in Geertz's formulation: 'man is an animal suspended in webs of significance he himself has spun' (Geertz 1973: 5). Dealing with Mountain Ok cosmology, we are thus dealing with meaning which is *conferred* on a sector of the world. With this perspective, our questions naturally focus on which meanings, for which purposes, with claims of validity for which sector – and not on explicating a coherent, albeit wrong, model of a reality out there supposedly entertained by a particular group. Likewise, we are invited to approach our subject with questions of how meaning is constructed and conferred, how the webs are spun, rather than merely what is the shape of the edifice so constructed.

Let me illustrate this mode of approach with a substantive example. I have identified the object of Ok cosmology above all as Nature: the life forms that surround the Ok in their mountain slope environment. One group of species of consuming interest to them are the screw-palms or pandanuses. What does the Baktaman sub-tradition have to say about pandanus, what are the meanings conferred and the webs of significance that are spun?

The Baktaman data have been summarized elsewhere (Barth 1975: 187ff). Most of what is 'said' is expressed in non-verbal idioms. Firstly, different pandanus species are classified together in one higher-order taxon, and are substituted ritually for each other, thereby invoking new associations which gain enhanced significance from being treated as covert and secret insights (cf. *ibid.*: 186). Further, a number of ritual contrivances are employed: emphatic juxtaposition, symbolic substitution, and the exhibition or creation of similarities in formal properties (colour, shape, function) to create and order other associations. By these means, a vast harmony of connotations is created connecting aspects of pandanus with other important objects and activities and these with each other.

Major elements, or statements, can be summarized as follows: Just as foraging cassowaries are attracted to some pandanus fruits, men are attracted to several other kinds of pandanus fruits and nuts. Pandanus and cassowary must be cooked with one separate set of fire-stones; pigs, taro and marsupials with another. Only initiation equals can eat pandanus together. The red pandanus fruit must be hollowed out with a gouge fashioned from a cassowary femur, almost indistinguishable from a human femur. The red pandanus fruit is phallic in shape and about a meter long. From the leaves covering this fruit as it develops, the fibres are extracted and used uniquely to produce two similar kinds of plaited rings, used to attach arrowheads to the arrow shafts, and to attach the phallocrypt to the male organ. Ancestral relics are kept in shrines made of pandanus leaf bases. At Mafom initiation, as we saw, shredded pandanus leaves are braided into the young men's hair and made into a wig with a 'male' and 'female' braid; the 'male' braid, and the novice's body, are painted red with paint containing pandanus juice. Dry pandanus leaves are used as tinder. In fire-making, the name of the small marsupial mouse (*ubir*) is secretly called at the climactic moment when fire is generated; this marsupial makes its nest of dried pandanus leaves. Whereas it is not the object of any other ritual observance, other than the special abstention of *not* being used as sacrifice in the temple, the most closely similar marsupial *eiraram* is officially regarded as vermin, but secretly given *in toto* to the ancestors as the supreme rite of sacrifice.

The meanings that are thus established are statements of particular associations and connections – or disjunctions. They are given special importance by the meta-premise of the secret cult: that things are not as they appear on the surface, not what you think – the really significant objects and connections in the world are those which are ritually shown you, or perhaps only hinted at, or from which you may even be shielded by the practice of even deeper secrets. The connections which compose the webs, or harmonies, arise in part in different contexts. Some are factual in the sense of being based on natural observations. Some are part of the everyday practice of correct custom, justified by a sense of rightness and order, as the separate cooking arrangements with separate fire-stones. Some are elementary parts of sacred idiom, as the use of pandanus leaves to construct shrines. Some are incorporated into the instructions given to novices on the solemn occasions when they are ritually authorized to assume new roles, e.g. when they are first allowed to prepare and

eat red pandanus fruit. Finally, only some of these associations and connections are made explicit – crossreferenced, so to speak – in the ritually most
salient contexts of the major initiations.

The extent and way in which pandanus is made thematically central in the
initiations of the different Mountain Ok sub-traditions in fact varies greatly.
The material is inadequate for systematic comparisons, but sufficient to document a wide range of variation: Among the Faiwolmin of Bolovip, second
degree (*ami-ban*) and third degree (*qown-ban*) initiations focus specifically on
pandanus of middle altitude and high altitude respectively, initiations for
which there are no equivalents among the Baktaman. From the Bimin-
Kuskusmin, Poole reports a Great Pandanus Rite unknown elsewhere, in
which *Kauun* and *Bokhuur* pandanuses are identified as 'female' and 'male'
respectively, and the ritual climax involves cannibalism of persons of the
opposite sex (Poole in Brown & Tuzin 1983).

But the purpose of this material was to bring us further in specifying the *kind*
of understanding that composes Ok cosmology by observing it in context. It
would clearly be a distortion to interpret these representations of pandanus
among the Baktaman as primarily objective statements about an empirical
world, with a view to practical science, of the type 'the *ubir* marsupial causes
fire' or 'a red pandanus wig will make you potent'. Invoking an analogy to
Western science, it would be more justified to look to Bohr's planetary model
for the atom: 'think of A as B'; 'your newly developed potency is as a glorious
red pandanus fruit, as a flying arrow' or 'the first tiny glow of fire in the tinder
must be protected like an *ubir* baby in its nest'. But even these renderings lean
towards our Western notions of cosmology in a way that is not fully warranted.
Admittedly, the Baktaman showed a material and practical interest in their
cosmology, and could be both pragmatic and outright mechanistic in their constructions of it. But I cannot see that perspective as the central, constitutive
one in the tradition of knowledge sustained by their rites. Thus, for example,
when I tried to ask just how sacrifices to the ancestral skull helped the taro gardens, some Baktaman suggested that the ancestor spirit was moved to travel
under ground to the garden and make the taro grow. But others immediately
dismissed this, apparently as naïve and too literal; and they would go no further
than to emphasize the force of the will of a benign ancestor.

Certainly, the non-verbal assertions made in these rituals leave the
mechanisms of connection entirely unexplored. Thus, the mechanisms cannot
be central to the knowledge that is being communicated. Setting ourselves the
impossible task of translating these assertions into a verbal idiom (cf. Barth
1975: 224f), a conservative rendering of the essential form of the statements
would be merely: 'When thinking of A, associate it with B', or in a perhaps
more precise form: 'Let A and B merge in so far as you should adopt a similar
attitude to them'. It would be to miss the function and force of this form of
statement to say merely that it is 'symbolic'. Besides the objection that all

71

statements, and all cognition, are perforce symbolic, idiomatic reading of 'symbolic' in English implies 'not to be taken really seriously'. The important insight, I would argue, is that Mountain Ok cosmology is not merely about a world out there, isolated from the self. More essentially, it provides a web of concepts, connections and identities whereby one's own attitudes and orientation to the various parts of the world are directed and moulded.

The significance of this distinction is enhanced by a brief excursion into some elements of psychoanalytic theory. Freud's construction of the unconscious (Freud 1900) is based on the concept of primary process, in contrast to the secondary process generally identified with logical thought. Primary process is fundamentally egocentric, because it is organized around subjective criteria, *viz*: what objects – percepts and actions – do in providing satisfaction to an infant. Secondary process is analytic in building its representations on the basis of a reality principle rather than a pleasure principle, and is associated with learning the practice of delayed gratification rather than to seek immediate drive gratification.

Noy (1969, 1979) reviews these concepts in the light of later developments in ego psychology, and seeks to construct the foundations for a psychology of art on these bases. He summarizes the main operations of primary process in a developmental sequence: condensation (whereby all objects associated with the same affective state are treated as a single element); displacement (whereby objects are distinguished, but can be freely displaced by one another within the affect-organized group); primary association (whereby objects are explored and grouped in terms of their different perceptual similarities of touch, colour, form, etc.); and symbolization (whereby displacement is confined to elements falling in a common subgroup in terms of primary association). His thesis is that these operations have a continued relevance for the self throughout life, and are not limited to an infantile stage or to incidents of regression to such a stage, or indeed to the subconscious. The mature ego has a twofold function: (1) to encounter reality in order to regulate drive discharge in consideration of objective reality (secondary process), and (2) to preserve self-continuity and identity by assimilating and integrating experience into the self (primary process).

The two processes of encountering reality and self-integration must proceed hand in hand, because in the healthy adult neither can function without the other . . . These two 'sets' of programs have to operate together, meaning that every input processed according to reality-orientated programs has to be 'translated' by passing through a second process of self-centred programs – and, vice versa, any activity originated by self-centred motivation has to be 'translated' from its self-centred organization through reality-oriented programs in order to be expressed as behaviour. (Noy 1969: 175)

Dream, fantansy and art make use of the primary process operations of condensation, displacement, primary association, and symbolization to construct the personal meanings whereby objects and events are integrated into wider

72

groups of experience and memory. This self-integration, argues Noy, does not only take place in the subconscious. As fantasy and a variety of similar mental activities it is also part of consciousness; moreover, it becomes intersubjective in modes of expression and communication such as play and art.

There is a striking parallel between the four operations of primary process outlined by Noy, and the means by which Ok cosmological representations are constructed (cf. pp.34f., 61f.). Likewise his emphasis on the self-integrating functions of these operations agrees very closely with what I can formulate, on the basis of an attempt at careful precision, as the essential content and thrust of the non-verbal statements about cosmological matters which are articulated in Mountain Ok ritual. Obeyesekere observes perceptively (1981: 165ff.) how in South Asian culture, there is a greater tolerance for fantasy and subjective imagery than in the West – thus the boy who is visited at night by his dead grandmother is regarded by others as especially gifted, not disturbed. As a result, Obeyesekere argues, pathways are established 'between id and ego whereby fantasy can come into open consciousness and the superego can tolerate its presence' (*ibid.*:167). Likewise, among the Mountain Ok, it is not a categorical failure of logical thought, but a closer hand-in-handedness of the operations of primary and secondary process which characterizes their cognitive style. Having drawn the analogy with South Asia, I should also emphasize a difference of some importance. We must remember the exceptional status of the men among the Mountain Ok who lead the rituals and articulate the imagery of this cosmology. They are in no sense the rather pathetic figures we meet in Obeyesekere's psychomantics; on the contrary, they could rightly think of themselves as the Renaissance giants of their society, masters of nearly the totality of their group's culture and controllers of all its sacred lore. In matters of cosmology, this assurance has fuelled their creativity in a tradition of knowledge that happens to be methodologically almost the obverse of our own. The core areas of Western cosmology have been built on a most single-minded application of description in terms of dichotomizing and hierarchical taxonomies, and generalization in terms of abstraction of similarities in relations of cause-and-effect. Ok cosmology has gone the opposite way. Given the high cultural valuation, especially in secret ritual, of modes of association which we in our culture allow only exceptionally gifted artists, Ok cosmology is built on descriptions governed by criteria of aptness of imagery, and generalization by assimilation or condensation. The resultant tradition of knowledge has its own dignity and force, very imperfectly captured by a narrowly 'cerebral' and abstract interpretation. Its main strength lies in how it directs and molds the person's subjective experience, and thus creates emotions and sensibilities that are harmonious with a vast structure of percepts and events in nature. I shall base my final attempt to explicate the dynamics of Mountain Ok cosmology as a tradition of knowledge on this model of its basic organization and mode of operation.

10

General and comparative perspectives

The various cosmological visions that we have been discussing compose a major part of the spiritual tradition of a materially simple neolithic society. It is not altogether straightforward to discern the presence of such a tradition, lacking as it is in the physical signposts around which civilizations organize their comparable systems of knowledge: the stately architecture, the fulltime specialists, the political luminaries they serve, the esoteric archives they maintain. In a rather similar situation among the Ndembu, Turner observed:

Gradually I became aware of a vast and complicated system of ceremonial practices going on around me somewhat as one picks out the skyline of a distant city in the growing dawn. It was an astonishing and enriching experience to note the contrast between the relatively simple and monotonous economic and domestic life of these hunters and hoe cultivators and the ordered arrangement and colourful symbolism of their religious life. (Turner 1967: 2).

The Ndembu, indeed, compose a population and occupy a territory roughly comparable in size to the sector of the Mountain Ok covered in the preceding discussion, and are in many ways also comparable in the profusion and force of their ritual life. Yet clearly, in major respects the two traditions differ, not only because the cultural contents they transmit are historically unrelated, but also because the traditions of knowledge are differently constituted. What are the dimensions of analysis which would capture and explain both the nature of the Mountain Ok achievement – its world view, the kind of understandings it provides, and the character of its productivity – and the differences that obtain between the Mountain Ok tradition, and other traditions of knowledge?

The preceding discussion has focussed on three gross components of Mountain Ok cosmology: (1) its social organization, (2) the material means by which it is communicated, and (3) the patterning of its contents, in terms of distribution, forms of coherence, and directions of marginal change. These must provide, it would seem to me, at least the provisional topology on which an anthropology of knowledge can build. The connections between social organization and content in a cultural tradition have most notably been explored by Redfield and his associates (Redfield 1956, Singer 1972, Marriott 1959, 1969). The connections between means of communication and content have more recently

Perspectives

received attention through Goody's stimulating discussion of literacy (Goody 1968, 1977).

Let us first reflect briefly on the Ok materials with respect to this latter theme. The evidence supports a thesis that the medium or code in which a body of knowledge is cast will tend to entail a definition of the nature of the object of knowledge, and will influence the kind of knowledge that is produced (above pp.67ff.). Ok cosmology focusses on Nature as its object, and the implicit concept of Nature which Ok cosmologists embrace, their idea of what reality is like, reflects properties of the ritual code in which their most authoritative cosmological statements are cast. The medium is one of metaphor, as in the manipulation of sacred concrete objects and ritual acts to generate statements about fertility, dependence, etc. This cultivation of metaphor leads to a basic multivocality of symbols. In this case, as in Goody's argument with respect to the effects of the historic development of literacy, it is not a question of postulating limits to what may be said, once you have completed a thought and master the medium. It is rather a question of where your thinking tends to lead you, when you are working in a particular medium. Thus Goody argues that the development of writing produces a novel durability of verbal statements, which separates the statement from its particular context and person, and obversely gives an essential simultaneity of many words which leads, for example, to the idea of making lists and inventories. Though Ok persons are perfectly able to develop such skills, as proved by their recent successful participation in a high-technology mining operation,[1] there is nothing in their traditional modes of communication which encourages the Ok to develop

---

[1] The capacity of untrained and pre-trained Ok villagers to function in a modern, high-technology organization has been put to the test through their individual participation as labour in the Ok Tedi mining operation in Wopkaimin territory. Since the discovery of gold and copper ore in the area in 1968, a growing number of Ok children have been enrolled in an Australian-based school system. As the construction phase, and later the extraction of ore, finally got under way in 1980, an appreciable number of mountain villagers have also been employed by the Ok Tedi Company, numbering 110 men in January 1982. The capacity of these youngsters and men to pass through the school system and to learn to participate in the Ok Tedi labour force respectively is remarkable. Yet, while engaged in a 'cultural impact study' of these phenomena (Barth and Wikan 1982) we became painfully aware of how unaccountable many of the processes in culture contact and change indeed are. Whereas a number of secondary effects on Ok life and activities were readily apparent, 'cultural impact' in the deeper sense of changes in the embraced conceptions and values of Ok villagers remained obscure. Essentially, I found no way in the imposed and regimented life of boarding school and labour camp to identify the extent and form in which components of Western culture had been adopted or embraced by Ok persons. Both in school and at work, such persons were simultaneously trained and controlled to a substantive set of knowledge and skills, the modalities of their expressions, and the contexts for their use. Returning individually to their village communities, the scope for them to practice or express new ideational impulses they brought with them likewise seemed highly restricted. How can an anthropologist then judge the meaning, value or import of new ideas for the actors themselves? A very deep and sensitive participation, of great intimacy and over long time, would seem to be required to capture the fleeting and tentative expressions of such discongruous, and potentially momentous, changes.

75

them. On the contrary, the use of concrete symbols in metaphor leads to an ordered and elaborated multivocality of symbols which tends to join multiple significances in unique clusters and make them seem immanent in objects. Combined with the pervasive practice of secrecy, this means that statements, and the Nature which the statements are about, take on some of the aspects of a cryptogram. Things are never merely, or really, what they appear to be. Again and again, participants in such a tradition will experience how deeper knowledge and insight reveal that something one thought was dirty is really clean, what one felt to be abhorrent is really valued and sacred, what was thought insignificant is pregnant with meaning. Thus the sacred symbols of the Mountain Ok are not only multivocal, but also deeply multivalent; and reality is best apprehended by a cultivation of mystery, not by a search for definitive truth.

It follows that deep knowledge in such a tradition is conceived as necessarily inexplicit – what we might idiomatically refer to as 'intuitive' or 'gut feeling' – and key concepts are usually characterized by their wordlessness (cf. Stanner 1960). I am not merely arguing for the existence of implicit structure. Hutchins, in an interesting analysis of Trobriand legal discourse and reasoning (Hutchins 1980), seems to demonstrate that although expression is by hyperbole, there is an unexplicated but constitutive unitary theory in terms of which the legal arguments are pursued – rather like the grammar of a spoken language. This may be correct in the particular case; but one cannot generally reason from the objective presence of a pattern in a cultural expression to the presence of an underlying, and causal, structure of thought. Vygotsky alerts us to one way in which the two can occur separately by demonstrating how the child uses 'because', 'if' and 'therefore' long before it grasps causal, conditional and implicative relations (cf. Hallpike 1979: 74). The syntax of speech can, in other words, be generated by a native speaker without command of the logical operations which seem constitutive of that syntax. Similarly, patterns in other cultural products may result from operations, or interactions, very different from the logical transformations which most economically generate those patterns. This should not lead to a resurrection of theories of pre-logical thought etc. – on the contrary, I am pleading for the recognition of positive achievements deriving from the potentialities of particular communicative forms. My thesis is that it would represent a distortion and impoverishment of Ok cosmology, and the kind of insight which this tradition of knowledge pursues, to reduce it to a unitary set of abstract and unambiguous propositions. The medium in which the knowledge is cast allows other and rich forms of understanding, and directs its practitioners in large part to pursue them. For the anthropologist to explore this richness it is necessary at the outset to have an open mind and, as an empirical question, enquire into what kind of knowledge is cultivated in the tradition, and in what praxis contents the knowledge is applied. I have suggested that Ok cosmological beliefs and concepts obtain their value and force from the way they bridge the gap for the individual between reality orientation (particularly toward Nature) and self integration. The capacity to perform this function I would see as closely dependent on the basic character of the medium in which authoritative communications in the tradition are cast, *viz*: a broad variety of multivocal and multivalent concrete symbols and acts.

Let us next reflect on the connections between social organization and the contents of the Ok tradition. Perhaps it would clarify the discussion if I specify somewhat further what I intend. I wish to pose questions regarding the contents of a tradition: what are the possible *kinds* of coherence and pattern for which we may search in the body of Ok cosmological knowledge and belief. The topic is usually conceived as a question of the 'integration' of a culture. If such integration is not merely asserted as the basis for a program of functional analysis, the anthropologist's procedure has been one of logical analysis and abstraction to find a generally valid basic structure of premises which orders the cultural materials in question. Another aspect of this procedure is the unquestioned assumption that the pattern and integration that prevails in a single individual's world view is of the same kind, and exhaustive of, that which might prevail in the culture of a local group.

My use of the concept of 'tradition' is part of an effort to break loose from this perspective and its assumptions (cf. Barth 1983). One way of putting it is to point out that culture is 'distributive' (Schwartz 1978). The distribution of the items of knowledge and ideas on the interacting parties in a population is a major feature of the organization of that body of knowledge and ideas; it is not only a matter of social structure but simultaneously a matter of cultural structure. It is self-evident that a particular pattern of social organization will produce and reproduce a particular pattern of distribution of knowledge and skills. Equally, a certain distribution of these cultural elements between persons motivates their interactions and exchanges, and thus animates a particular social organization and infuses it with its constitutive qualities. Again and again in social science, it has proved useful to distinguish these two aspects of system, so as to rejoin them in a dynamic model. Thus, Durkheim (1893 [1970]) showed how the organization of the division of labour in a society entails and reproduces a particular distribution of knowledge and skills between its members, and how this distribution structures the interactions of persons and thereby generates the characteristic form of (organic) cohesion in that society. In the study of gender, we have come to understand how a culturally standardized articulation of gender roles will canalize a person's experience of cross- and same-gender interactions and thereby shape his or her conception of gender identity – and equally, how the desire to realize these culturally cherished gender identities brings people together in that patterned interaction (MacCormack & Strathern 1980). Likewise, the analysis of ethnicity has shown how existing cultural differences between two or more

77

interacting groups can lead to their agonistic demarcation – but also how cultural differentia are developed and produced, to serve as banners of identity when confronting groups are mobilizing (Barth 1967). In similar fashion, I have tried to identify both the way in which Ok social organization (in gender, initiation sets, clan divisions, etc.) presupposes a pattern in the distribution of knowledge and ideas, and the way in which the activities which constitute that social organization generate and reproduce the distribution of ideas in the population, the contents and forms of coherence in their collective cultural tradition, and the marginal changes which take place within it as a consequence of such patterns and processes.

In the Ok case, the salient features of social organization are four: (1) The segmentation of the population into small, localized and mutually rather suspicious local groups. (2) The differentiations of gender and initiation step within each such group. (3) The specialized role of initiator as the authoritative knower and revealer of secrets. (4) The pulsation in the modality of cosmological knowledge between long periods of secrecy and non-communication, and concentrated bursts of public manifestation and revelation.

I have already argued at length how these features combine to provide a pervasive impetus to creativity and modification of tradition on the part of initiators, despite a native epistemology that sees transmission from previously living ancestors as the only source of knowledge. But they also have profound effects on the nature of audiences to such communication. The organization of gender and initiations provides a multilayered systematic differentiation of the keys to interpreting communications about cosmology that are held by different members of every local group and audience. Add to this the range of variation between individuals in cosmological interest and symbolic sensitivity and imagination, exacerbated by the ambience of danger-and-importance permeating these ritual events, and one can recognize the heterogeneity of even small audiences in these very small-scale societies.

Since our questions concern the reproduction of tradition, we need to focus on the communicative *consequences* of events. This means that we cannot simply treat each ritual in isolation as a cultural object, a text containing a message. The communicative consequences of Ok cosmological messages are not retrieved by an account of what has been encoded by the initiator, as if it were embedded in the shape of the message. When different recipients hold different keys, they will learn different things from the event, and a schema which represents the process as one of expressing and transmitting bits of knowledge is inadequate. The question is what will be induced in the various participants and audiences to a communicative event: Ok rituals need to be understood more like happenings, and less like ciphers. This is, of course, a position widely adopted in modern art and art criticism; but I have not been able to find theoretically and methodologically useful statements of the position and its implications for a more rigorous attempt to analyse the effective

78

contents of communication. Yet this is hardly a reason to adopt other, more systematically articulated but less appropriate, positions. Again, we must give primacy to getting our ontology right.

The position I have adopted has two components: (1) Creativity is not inside the initiator, but springs from his relations with his surroundings. This is significantly structured by a social organization which provides him with (a) an audience of novices with a certain range of knowledge and sensibilities (b) a task of suddenly and dramatically making a spellbinding mystery of nature and fertility manifest, and (c) a medium which offers a range of moving metaphors and associations for this purpose. My other premise is (2) That which is created is not a text, a 'work' of art or science, but a transformation of a group of young persons into men who think and feel about – sense – nature and themselves in certain ways and with certain imagery. My task is to give an account of this social context, the events that unfold, and the consequences they have, not to give an 'interpretation' of a cultural product.

For this purpose, I focus on process: the aggregate consequences of events of communication. We also need to recognize and connect correctly the different levels of system: persons, local communities, and the Ok region as a whole. I have emphasized the diversity of persons and keys in a local community, and the consequent range of understandings generated from a single ritual performance. But it would be to underestimate the force of native cosmologists and the initiations they stage to exaggerate this range and ignore the homogenizing which their instruction and transmission effect. The evidence indicates that male cohorts moving through joint initiations obtain a body of generally shared items of cosmological knowledge, and a general area of common sensibilities and intuitions. My point is, this will be a movable, impressionable and everchanging inheritance, only approximately shared in the group; it generates not a unified system of knowledge agreed by all, but a range of understandings sufficient so its members can be moved by the same symbols and thoughts. Many of the particular conceptions that are entertained within the local group will be only loosely connected, and carry unresolved ambiguities and enigmatic contradictions. Particularly such unresolved areas will tend to be the focus of intellectual, symbolic work (cf. the wild boar among the Baktaman, above p.35 and Barth 1975: 240f.), and will be subject to marginal reshaping by the creative visions of the more interested and more articulate. The kind of coherence that will characterize the cosmological tradition in any one locality will thus be intuitive, agglutinative, and variable in its nature, rather than logical and deductive.

Not so the variations *between* localities: we cannot picture the coherence that obtains in the Ok tradition as a whole in such terms. Quite clearly, the total stream of Ok cosmological speculation confronts us with a field of raucous variation. Does this variation merely represent an unshapely chaos, or does it have an underlying pattern, a coherence of some kind? If it has a pattern, what

kind of coherence does this pattern reflect? Is it a pattern of contrastive mark-
ings only, by which local temples signal their distinctness, producing a
checkerboard of contrasts? Or is it the precipitate of a battle between competing interpreters locked in theological debate – a kind of proliferating scholas-
ticism? Or is perhaps the range of world views somehow fitted to, and controlled by, a range of ecological and demographic determinants? Or must we
seek for a more general coherence, a family resemblance of basic type,
overlaid by branching proliferation? The kind of pattern for which one
searches should on the one hand be determined by empirical data: we should
try to discover the ways in which the variation is patterned. Further, it should
be explicable in processual terms: the events of religious practice, and the
marginal changes that arise from that practice, should provide plausible
sources for the kinds of regularity and variations that are found.

The model of cosmological communication and innovation which I have
presented is one that would generate an interplay of (largely divergent) processes of individual creativity and modification and (largely convergent)
cross-influence and borrowing arising from compelling ideas and charismatic
initiators. Such processes should generate regional trends over time, but also
some discontinuous variation and incompatible syntheses in different parts of
the region. The variation found at any one time in the cosmological visions of
different Ok groups can thus, I would suggest, be understood as the precipitate
of a culture history of changeability – from diffusion and innovation – within
chains of transmission located in each temple and each men's house; here producing parallelism and convergence, there cumulative divergence. Where the
ideas or idioms found in two such local sub-traditions have diverged strongly,
direct borrowing is probably minimal even if occasional intervisiting takes
place (as between Baktaman and Bimin-Kuskusmin, see p.36). Yet ideas and
stimuli may still move between them, through interlinking and intermediate
third parties (for example into the ritual centre in Telefolmin, and out again in
new directions). With such stimuli moving widely in the Ok network, there is
thus no reason to assume a progressive branching, and loss of coherence, in the
Ok cosmological tradition as a whole. We have here located, I would argue, in
Ok social organization a mutually reinforcing combination of features which
may be understood to generate the characteristic cacophony of diverse visions
that coexist within the broad current of Ok cosmology.

At an earlier point in this essay, I loosely used the image of 'debate' for the
relationship between some alternative conceptions in Ok cosmology (above,
p.18). I would not wish to give the impression that this image provides the
best and generally valid model of the processes involved. We have no basis to
assume that different conceptions are generally confronted and pressed
towards resolution or abandonment. What takes place is much more like a –
perhaps suspicious and fearful – search for inspiration and enlightenment. It
might be clarifying to draw some comparisons to other, drastically differently

organized, traditions of knowledge, since the different processes that characterize them produce very different kinds of coherence and very different trajectories of change from those which I have identified in Ok traditon.

A comparison with indigenous Indian civilization is instructive. Redfield developed an account of the distinctive, qualitative features of Indian civilization as a cultural system with reference to its organization in a coexisting and interdependent 'Great Tradition' and a multiplicity of 'Little Traditions'. The former is carried and elaborated by a scholarly and reflective elite focussing on a shared literary heritage, the latter are represented by common people sharing local cultures. Perhaps most clearly in Marriott's essays (1959, 1969), the resulting content of the traditions, and the dialogue between them, have been depicted in terms of channels of communication, peopled by specialists of various kinds. The work of these specialists entails a stepwise transformation of cultural materials in both directions: parochialization when ideas from the Great Tradition become anchored and assimilated to local imagery, universalization when local ideas are identified with, or allowed to develop into, elements in the Great Tradition. The account thus suggests a model of processes which give direction and coherence to a vast field of intellectual activity, and in terms of which the content and forms of coherence in Indian culture may be grasped. Whether the force which animates this process is seen as struggle within a social heirarchy or a search for enlightenment, the pervasive Sanscritization it produces will tend to govern the kinds of regional variations that occur, and the broad directions of change, in a dynamics very different from that exemplified by the Ok.

Confrontation and resolution of divergent views through debate, on the other hand, is generally regarded as constitutive of the traditions of knowledge which we accept as scholarly and scientific. Let us again use our immediate familiarity with the British school of social anthropology to explore in somewhat closer detail the extent to which such a process of debate seems to be formative of the coherence that obtains within the tradition of British social anthropology.

Superficially, the social organization of anthropology in British universities may appear quite similar to my description of that of Ok initiators and temple congregations. Seen from within the tradition, the teachings of its local Departments and factions during the 1950s and '60s may also have been experienced as quite cacophonic. Leach (1984) emphasizes the differences between its leading figures in terms of backgrounds and philosophical positions. And, finally, direct confrontations across the major lines of division were rarer than the infrastructure of seminars, meetings, and journals might lead one to expect; when they did occur, they were sometimes uneasily felt to be slightly unseemly. Yet, we should not be misled by appearances and gross frequencies. Within each department and each class, much instruction took the form of critiques, i.e. were fragments of debate with an absent alter. In the local milieus, incremental change took place through a failure of effective persuasion of students in the internal fora of communication, resulting in incidents of successful influence across the institutional divisions between lines of teaching and transmission. A major factor in creating these forms of coherence was the fact that British social anthropologists addressed themselves to a common body of (everchanging) theory and knowledge – they all had the same books on their shelves (*ibid.*: 21), read the same journals, and demanded of their students a command of the same growing and changing body of literature. I would judge this to be the major factor that gave coherence to the British school, from its emergence to dominance in the thirties to its eclipse in the sixties. In terms of the very general concepts of the preceding discussion, it thus would seem that a somewhat oblique form of debate was indeed formative of its coherence, and that the tradition was organized on the premise that universalization was every scholar's overriding program, and the basis even for the local perpetuation of the tradition. We thus see a very different configuration of organization and processes than those exemplified in the Hindu tradition, and the Ok tradition. Where British social anthropology resulted in a cumulative, collective movement temporarily canalized by a minor formative paradigm – Hindu civilization would seem to produce a perpetual dialogue over some relatively stable, highly elaborate themes, while the Ok tradition hones old metaphors and gives wings to new ones in an eternally changing and bubbling witch's cauldron.

11

Some reflections on theory and method

In this exposition of variations in cosmology among neighbouring Ok groups, I have gone into the specifics of beliefs and modes of organization only with the analytical purpose of discovering and illustrating the processes at work in them, and not so as to map them out and depict them as structural wholes. This point is essential to the theoretical and methodological position I have adopted, and might usefully be discussed in some of its aspects.

My point can most vividly be highlighted by contrast. Tambiah, with characteristic clarity, has described his methodology in an instructive structuralist exercise as follows: 'My discovery procedure is not in "causal" terms as this is conventionally understood but in terms of revealing analogical structures that are embedded in the ethnographic accounts scrutinized, structures that are related to one another by parallelisms, inversions, oppositions, transpositions etc.' (Tambiah 1983: 172). My discovery procedure, on the other hand, has been to focus on interactional events, construct my description of such events as a model of a process, and then consider whether the results of the recurrent operations of such a process would be those aggregate patterns which the ethnographies reveal. Alternatively, the sequence can be reversed and move from the discovery of a pattern in a cultural manifestation or an institutionalized form and to the search for a process which can generate it. In this latter case the difference from the methods of structuralism may appear superficially slight, at least initially; but they are pervasive in that the pattern is not treated as a thing in itself, to be compared to other things, but rather to be read as tracks are read, as results that are left behind by something that has passed and may be identified from the particular features of its tracks. Bateson describes a similar progression of investigation and model building as a zigzag sequence of steps between models of 'process' and models of 'form' (Bateson 1980: 204ff, esp. p.209). This moves the attention away from comprehensive depictions of the edifice of institutions and collective representations, and focuses more on praxis, and the saliency of experiences generated by that praxis. Of particular interest are possible disparities between collective representations on the one hand, and individual experience and thought on the other, or differences between received tradition and its reproduction. Very

83

simply: we expand our understanding of this tradition of cosmology, not by construing more order *in* it, but by better accounting for its production.

This is intended as a call to focus on reproduction and change, in the contexts where events can be studied (cf. Barth 1967), and not to attempt to reconstruct the grand sweep of history or phylogeny, where the empirical processes involved cannot be observed. It is particularly important to avoid the naïveté of posing the *tabula rasa* case as the prototype or test case for such a model of process and form. Popper helpfully formulates the epistemological credo that 'knowledge is always a modification of earlier knowledge' (Popper & Eccles, 1984: 425). The anthropology of any particular tradition of knowledge should thus above all be asked to account for how certain compositions and distributions of knowledge are (re)produced and modified, *in casu* how the processes of codification, transmission and creativity in Ok cosmology generate the pattern of variation which the ethnographies record, not how the first bit of knowledge might be created. This entails a marginalist perspective: how might small but cumulative changes reshape the face of vast collective institutions?

The perspective thus adopted differs from that of structuralism in a number of its ontological assumptions or implications. Either set of assumptions can be more or less appropriate depending on the nature of the phenomena we are investigating; and it seems to me essential that we strive for naturalism and adopt a critical scepticism to our imputations – regardless of their methodological convenience. At several points in the preceding essay I have stressed the need for 'getting our ontology right'. I shall now briefly summarize some respects in which I believe the perspective adopted here to have a greater validity than the ontological assumptions that flourish in the lee of structuralism, when applied to cultural phenomena.

Perhaps most fundamentally, I have avoided the mode of representation where any particular cultural manifestation is transformed to an abstraction – 'culture' – which is treated as internally homogeneous and shared, and externally bounded. Depicting the (degree of) coherence between different ideas and expressions does not in this account depend on the template of a jigsaw puzzle; the perpetually interactional and contingent character of cultural phenomena is not expurgated from their description. Nor does the analysis prejudge the aspects of meaning of cultural items in terms of a particular theory of language or of binary representation: the ultimate appeal is to communicative effort and effect, not to (the analyst's) logical premise.

The focus has been on cosmology as a living tradition of knowledge – not as a set of abstract ideas enshrined in collective representations. This allows us to see the events taking place in a tradition as incidents of the very processes that shape that tradition. We may look for the manifest sources of metaphor and symbol in the concrete contexts and encounters that take place; we may trace the practical effects of the media of expression, and the social organization of

84

communication, on the changing content of the tradition. To interpret the evidence correctly, great attention must be given to the context in which these processes are embedded. For one thing, the plausible sources and correlates of ideas, and the nature of coherence in a tradition, will differ under different conditions of existence for that tradition; and this can only be appreciated if the expressions which compose it are correctly depicted with regard to the social and communicative loci in which they occur. We have here been concerned to explore cosmological variation in the autochthonous traditions of an, until recently, very isolated society. An exploration of meanings in the folk tradition of a society which has long been incorporated in the economic and political world system would have had to proceed along very different lines of search, even if the formal expressions – the idioms, rites and myths – appeared superficially like those here discussed for the Ok. Again, a third set of linkages would have to be explored if I were to represent the cosmology, or any other set of ideas, currently entertained by those Ok who have attended school in Tabubil and presently participate in the Ok Tedi mining operations (cf. my observations on p.75, fn.1).

Likewise, I have argued that the contents of Ok rites, and their import, cannot be adequately understood without equal attention to the many-year-long periods of latency during which the initiator shrouds them in the cloak of secrecy and taboo. My general thesis is that an account of a cultural expression which fails to specify such particulars as social organization, communicative media and periodicity is in danger of entirely misrepresenting the import of that expression. Meaning is not embedded in the form of an expression alone, and does not become transparent by the most elegant analysis of that form; it can only be interpreted when it is located in a social organization and a praxis of communication.

This leads to my third point. The analyses pursued here have emphasized the place of elements in the context of social situation, juxtaposition, and praxis more than the place of the element in the context of an abstract logical system. This runs counter to two common premises in our own scholarly tradition of knowledge: namely that an increase in abstraction represents an increase in truth value, and that knowledge should be integrated into a universal science. Specifications of situational context therefore tend to be disvalued, as failures of abstraction and evidence of inadequate generalization; whereas the logically clean localization of a representation within an abstract typology or system is hailed as the crowning act of analysis. But with the complex and prolific materials on which anthropologists are asked to report, this provides misleading guidelines and encourages a form of analysis where most of the vital data are given in the prolix prose of description, only to be whittled away through a structural analysis that leaves us with a stark, syntactic schema as its final result.

Together with an attention to praxis and context, I would argue for a greater commitment to the stuff of other cultural traditions in our analyses. We should make greater effort to let our discoveries shape our science. Anthropologists are strong on using conceptions from the other cultural traditions we are studying as a means to transcend our own categories – but we tend subsequently to domesticate these ideas by re-integrating them through abstraction into our pre-established anthropology. By giving more integrity to the context of praxis in which these concepts from other cultures are embedded, we can expand our horizons. This analysis of Ok thought has thus radically changed my own ideas of what can be the object of a cosmology, and the way our concepts may serve to mediate between reality and self as much as between objective constructs. In this, I am merely reflecting strivings shared by many colleagues. Let Schneider's recent disquiet over the appropriate terms in which to conceptualize Yapese 'descent groups' (Schneider 1984) serve as an illustration of a sustained attempt, from another methodological perspective, to pursue such a program. Much contemporary anthropology, however, pursues a paradigm which militates against such transcendence.

Finally, the analysis I have pursued depends on a conception of individual/ society and particular expression/collective representation which is somewhat at odds with that generally accepted as dogma in much social anthropology. Thus, it has long been a convention in British social anthropology to dismantle the individual into (1) a private, unique and psychic component and (2) a social person composed of the statuses through which the individual is a participant in society. This goes with making the private and 'unique' into an inaccessible black box assigned a vast and unspecified range of properties, leaving the social person a too simplified and therefore barren field for producing new insights into human existence. I urge that we rather recognize the penetration of society deep into the privacy and psyche of the individual, and that we acknowledge how much of every individual is out there, dispersed in his or her previous and current relationships with others. If we do so we will not so quickly abdicate before the 'unique' but try to reduce its place in our description of people's acts, orientations, intentions and understandings. Thereby we may also avoid mystifying creativity and that which is created, but rather stretch our discipline to capture far more of the flow of interaction in terms which make it accessible to our description and reasoning.

The other aspect of this precept concerns our handling of the particular cultural expression: a performance, a spell recitation, a painted skull. I have been particularly stimulated by Obeyesekere to avoid a rigid dichotomization of private symbols vs. collective representation, and sought instead to place more aspects of expressions in the gray zone of subjectification, externalization, and culture-in-the-making. This also allows us to let these cultural expressions retain their intimate linkage with their creators, and be treated as part of perfectly fathomable social interaction. In structuralism, on the contrary, there has been a tendency to treat such expressions as dismembered objects, living a life of their own independent of their producers. There is an aspect of truth in such representations also, particularly for some cultural products in some traditions of knowledge – yet even there, the conception militates against any contextualized description and analysis of creativity and the production of symbols and knowledge.

Now to put the two preceding paragraphs together, so as to depict the Ok cosmologist as an individual embedded in social relations engaged in producing his particular expression or representation. We must locate these events in the context of a tradition, in an environment of social relations and available communications technology. Moreover, we must ascribe an adequate dynamics to a system composed of such parts. Einstein is reported to have remarked how 'My pencil is cleverer than I' (Popper and Eccles 1984: 208). I read this to say that creativity can only be understood as an interaction between the parts of a dynamic system; and nothing can be expected to spring ready-made from the forehead of the philosopher. The above essay on Ok cosmologies and cosmologists has above all been an attempt to relate the form and content of the aggregate tradition to the means of transmission and creativity of persons located in that tradition.

In doing so, I have attempted to meet my own requirement of striving towards naturalism. Like most of us, I assume that there is a real world out there – but that our representations of that world are constructions. People create and apply these cultural constructions in a struggle to grasp the world, relate to it, and manipulate it through concepts, knowledge and acts. In the process, reality impinges; and the events that occur consequently are not predicated by the cultural system of representations employed by the people, though they may largely be interpretable within it. A people's way of life is thus not a closed system, contained within their own cultural constructions. That part of the real world on which we as anthropologists need to focus is composed of this widest compass: a natural world, a human population with all its collective and statistical social features, and a set of cultural ideas in terms of which these people try to understand and cope with themselves and their habitat. It is insufficient to delimit the object of anthropological study to the study of these ideas, collective representations, or cultural forms: we need to locate them in a system wider than that which the culture itself encompasses, so as to be able to record the praxis of a way of life and ask what people do in the world they inhabit. An hermeneutic or other interpretative program is thus not alone sufficiently comprehensive to serve our purpose. The anthropology of knowledge must encompass three spheres, each embracing the previous one, *viz*: native concepts and representations, the world as constituted by these concepts, and the real world of which this social and cultural construction forms a part.

This may seem a very ambitious program, and touches two central paradoxes in modern anthropological epistemology: (1) the necessity of participation and interaction to obtain data on society and culture, which militates against the constitution of 'society' and 'culture' as objects of observation separated from the observer; and (2) the logical hierarchy that seems implied in making a whole system of knowledge, i.e. a culture, an object of knowledge within another system of knowledge, i.e. anthropology.

Neither of these paradoxes are irresolvable, unless we demand of our own tradition that it provide exhaustive description of the real world, and final truth. There should be no logical or practical bar to doing what anthropologists indeed do: learning some native concepts and participating in native praxis, and thereupon exploring and reporting on features of the world as constituted by these concepts – compared to that constituted by the anthropologist's own set of concepts. Inadequate as such an account will be, because of the richness of native knowledge and concepts and the diversity of praxis, there is no theoretical limit to its improvement.

Likewise, I would argue that in trying to grasp the real world (containing other peoples and their conception of the world) through a set of concepts, anthropologists are doing nothing else than what numbers of other cultural traditions are doing, except in directing more discriminating attention to the concepts used by others, and the contrast between the perceptions obtained by the use of different concepts. We need not assert that our (account of the) world is the true world, only that our account can be improved; and we need not claim that our tradition of knowledge is of a different order from those which we include in our world, i.e. in our object of study. We may indeed include our own tradition in the compass of our object, and will find that we have ways of accumulating and aggregating observations so we can be surprised by discoveries, also in respect to our own discipline. All we need to believe is that we are developing theory and method which enhance our ability to see and reflect on how cultural traditions cope with the task of understanding the world – on other premises and with perhaps a narrower focus than that which we have, through the efforts of our predecessors, managed to achieve.

These remarks provide the general, theoretical foundations on the basis of which I feel we should broaden our compass in the study of cultural traditions as compared to what is practiced in several schools of social anthropology today. My remarks, however, do not so much spring out of the preceding analysis of Ok cosmologies as accompany it, and provide a general argument for my adoption of the discovery procedures of which I have made use. While the analysis of Ok cosmologies and the processes whereby they change thus does not stand and fall with the validity of these reflections, I would rather suggest that any satisfaction generated by that analysis might justify the consideration of the general points briefly formulated in these last paragraphs.

Bibliography

Barnes, J.A. 1962 African models in the New Guinea Highlands. *Man* 62: 5–9
Barth, F. 1966 *Models of Social Organization*. Royal Anthropological Institute Occasional Paper No.23 (Republished in F. Barth: *Process and Form in Social Life*. London: Routledge & Kegan Paul 1981)
1967 On the study of social change. *American Anthropologist* Vol.69
1971 Tribes and intertribal relations in the Fly headwaters. *Oceania* Vol.41 No.3
1973 Descent and marriage reconsidered *in* J. Goody ed.: *The Character of Kinship*. Cambridge: Cambridge University Press
1975 *Ritual and Knowledge among the Baktaman of New Guinea*. Oslo: Universitetsforlaget, New Haven: Yale University Press
1983 *Sohar: Culture and Society in an Omani Town*. Baltimore: The Johns Hopkins University Press
Barth, F. ed. 1969 *Ethnic Groups and Boundaries*. Oslo: Universitetsforlaget
1978 *Scale and Social Organization*. Oslo: Universitetsforlaget
Barth, F. and U. Wikan 1982 Cultural Impact of the Ok Tedi Project. *Report, Institute of Papua New Guinea Studies* (mimeo.)
Bateson, G. 1980 *Mind and Nature: A Necessary Unity*. Glasgow: Fontana
Berkovitch, E. 1982 *A regional perspective on the narrative traditions of the Min peoples of Papua New Guinea*. Institute of PNG Studies (mimeo)
Brown, P. and D. Tuzin (eds) 1983 *The Ethnography of Cannibalism*. Washington: Society for Psychological Anthropology
Brunton, R. 1980a Misconstrued order in Melanesian religion. *Man* (N.S.) Vol.15 No.1
1980b 'Correspondence'. *Man* (N.S.) Vol.15 No.4, pp.734–5
Craig, B. 1981 *Report of Mountain Ok field survey*. Anthropology Department, P.N.G. National Museum (ms.)
Darwin, Sir Charles 1843 *Narrative of the Surveying Voyages of H.M.S. Adventure and Beagle* (The Voyage of the Beagle. London: The Amalgamated Press 1905 edition)
1871 *The Descent of Man and Selection in Relation to Sex*. (The Origin of Species and the Descent of Man, Modern Library Edition)
de Lepervanche, M. 1967–8 Descent, residence and leadership in the New Guinea Highlands. *Oceania* Vol.38: 134–58 and 163–89
Durkheim, E. 1970 *The Division of Labour in Society*. Glencoe Illinois: Free Press (first published 1893)
Firth, R. 1959 Problem and assumption in an anthropological study of religion. *Journal of The Royal Anthropological Institute* Vol.90

89

Bibliography

Freud, S. 1900 *The Interpretation of Dreams* (Vols.4 & 5 of The Standard Edition of the Complete Psychological Works of Sigmund Freud. London: Hogarth)

Gardner, D.S. 1983 Performativity in ritual: the Mianmin case. *Man* (N.S.) Vol.18 No.2

Geertz, C. 1973 *The Interpretation of Cultures*. New York: Basic Books Inc.

Gell, A. 1980 'Correspondence'. *Man* (N.S.) Vol.15 No.4, pp.735–7

Gilsenan, M. 1977 'Review' of F. Barth: *Ritual and Knowledge among the Baktaman of New Guinea. RAIN* No.18 pp.12–13

Goody, J. 1977 *The Domestication of the Savage Mind*. Cambridge: Cambridge University Press

Goody, J. (ed.) 1968 *Literacy in Traditional Societies*. Cambridge: Cambridge University Press

Hallpike, C.R. 1979 *The Foundations of Primitive Thought*. Oxford: Clarendon Press

Herdt, G.H. (ed.) 1982 *Rituals of Manhood: Male Initiation in Papua New Guinea*. Berkeley: Univ. of California Press

Hutchins, E. 1980 *Culture and Inference: A Trobriand Case Study*. Cambridge, Mass.: Harvard Univ. Press

Hyndman, D.C. 1979 *Wopkaimin Subsistence: Cultural Ecology in the New Guinea Highland Fringe*. Thesis, University of Queensland

　　1982 Biotope gradient in a diversified New Guinea subsistence system. *Human Ecology* Vol.10 No.2

Johnson, R. 1981 'Correspondence'. *Man* (N.S.) Vol.16 No.3, pp.472–4

Jones, B.A. 1980 *Consuming Society: Food and Illness among the Faiwol*. Thesis, University of Virginia

Jorgensen, D. 1980 What's in a name: The meaning of meaninglessness in Telefolmin. *Ethos* Vol.8 No.4

　　1981 'Correspondence'. *Man* (N.S.) Vol.16 No.3, pp.470–2

　　1982 Mirroring nature? Men's and women's models of conception in Telefolmin (mimeo)

　　1984 The clear and the hidden: Person, self and suicide among the Telefolmin of Papua New Guinea. *Omega* Vol.12 No.2

　　n.d. The answer to death is life: The Telefol response to mortality. (Mimeo)

Juillerat, B. 1980 'Correspondence'. *Man* Vol.15 No.4, pp.732–4

Keesing, R.M. 1982 *Kwaio Religion*. New York: Columbia Univ. Press

Kuper, A. 1983 *Anthropology and Anthropologists: The modern British School* (revised ed.). London: Routledge & Kegan Paul

La Fontaine, J. 1977 The power of rights. *Man* (N.S.) Vol.12 No.314

Leach, E.R. 1954 *Political Systems of Highland Burma*. London: Bell & Sons

　　1967 Virgin Birth. *Proceedings of the Royal Anthropological Institute of Great Britain and Ireland for 1966*

　　1982 *Social Anthropology*. Glasgow: Fontana

　　1984 Glimpses of the unmentionable in the history of British Social Anthropology. *Annual Review in Anthropology* Vol.13

Lévi-Strauss, C. 1966a *The Savage Mind*. London: Weidenfeld & Nicholson (1962)

　　1966b *Du Miel aux Cendres*. Paris: Plon

Lewis, G. 1980 *Day of Shining Red: An Essay on Understanding Ritual*. Cambridge: Cambridge Univ. Press

MacCormack, C. and M. Strathern (eds) 1980 *Nature, Culture and Gender*. Cambridge: Cambridge University Press

Bibliography

Marriott, McK. 1959 Changing channels of cultural transmission in Indian civilization *in* V.F. Ray, ed.: *Intermediate Societies, Social Mobility and Communication*. Seattle: American Ethnological Society
1969 Little communities in an indigenous civilization *in* Marriott ed.: *Village India*. Chicago: University of Chicago Press
Maybury-Lewis, D. 1960 The analysis of dual organizations: A methodological critique. *Bijdragen tot de Taal-, Land- en Volkenkunde*, Deel 116
Nadel, S.F. 1951 *The Foundations of Social Anthropology*. London: Cohen & West
Noy, P. 1969 A revision of the psychoanalytic theory of the primary process. *International Journal of Psycho-Analysis* Vol.50
1979 Form creation in art: An ego-psychological approach to creativity. *Psychoanalytic Quarterly* Vol.48
Naess, A. 1982 *Hvilken verden er den virkelige?* Oslo: Universitetsforlaget
Obeyesekere, G. 1981 *Medusa's Hair*. Chicago: Univ. of Chicago Press
Poole, F.J.P. 1976 *The Ais Am: An Introduction to Male Initiation Ritual among the Bimin-Kuskusmin of the West Sepik District, Papua New Guinea* (Vols.1–5). Thesis, Cornell University
1982 The ritual forging of identity: Aspects of person and self in Bimin-Kuskusmin male initiation *in* G.H. Herdt (ed.): *Rituals of Manhood*. Berkeley: Univ. of California Press
1984 Symbols of substance: Bimin-Kuskusmin models of procreation, death, and personhood. *Mankind* Vol.14 No.3
n.d. Veils of illusion, kernels of truth: Secrecy and revelation in Bimin-Kuskusmin ritual *in* D.W. Jorgensen & E.G. Schwimmer, eds.: *Ritual Secrecy*. Toronto: Univ. of Toronto Press
Poole, F.J.P. and G.H. Herdt (eds.) 1982 Sexual Antagonism, Gender and Social Change in Papua New Guinea. Special Issue Series, *Social Analysis* No.12
Popper, K. and J.C. Eccles 1984 *Self and its Brain*. London: Routledge & Kegan Paul
Pouwer, J. 1964 A social system in the Star mountains *in* J.B. Watson, ed.: 'New Guinea. The Central Highlands'. *American Anthropologist* Vol.66 No.4, Part II. Special Publication
Redfield, R. 1956 *Peasant Society and Culture: An Anthropological Approach to Civilization*. Chicago: University of Chicago Press
Ricoeur, P. 1978 *Rule of Metaphor: Multidisciplinary Studies of the Creation of Meaning in Language*. London: Routledge & Kegan Paul
Rivers, W.H.R. 1924 *Social Organization*. London: Routledge
Schneider, D.M. 1984 *A Critique of the Study of Kinship*. Ann Arbor: Univ. of Michigan Press
Schwartz, T. 1978 The size and shape of a culture *in* F. Barth (ed.): *Scale and Social Organization*. Oslo: Universitetsforlaget
Singer, M. 1972 *When a Great Tradition Modernizes. An Anthropological Approach to Indian Civilization*. London: The Pall Mall Press
Southwold, M. 1979 Religious belief. *Man* (N.S.) Vol.14 No.4
Stanner, W.E.H. 1960 On aboriginal religion II. *Oceania* Vol.30 No.4
Strathern, A. 1972 *One Father, one Blood: Descent and Group Structure among the Melpa People*. Canberra: Australian National University Press
Strathern, M. 1981 Self-interest and social good: Some implications of Hagen gender imagery *in* S.B. Ortner & H. Whitehead (eds.): *Sexual Meanings*. Cambridge: Cambridge University Press

Bibliography

Swadling, P. 1983 *How Long have People been in the Ok Tedi Impact Region?* P.N.G. National Museum Record No.8

Tambiah, S.J. 1983 On flying witches and flying canoes: the coding of male and female values *in* J.W. Leach and E. Leach: *The Kula: New Perspectives on Massim Exchange*. Cambridge: Cambridge University Press

Turner, V. 1967 *The Forest of Symbols: Aspects of Ndembu Ritual*. Ithaca: Cornell University Press

Weber, M. 1949 *The Methodology of the Social Sciences*. Translated and edited by E.A. Shils & H.A. Finch. Glencoe, Illinois: The Free Press (orig. published 1904)

Weiner, A.B. 1982 Sexuality among the anthropologists: Reproduction among the informants *in* F.J.P. Poole & G.H. Herdt, eds.: 'Sexual Antagonism, Gender, and Social Change in Papua New Guinea'. *Social Analysis* Vol.12, Special Issue Series

Wheatcroft, W. 1976 *The Legacy of Afekan: Culture Symbolic Interpretations of Religion among the Tifalmin of New Guinea*. Thesis, University of Chicago

Index

Index

94

Index

Cambridge Studies in Social Anthropology

Editor: Jack Goody

97